Being in Ministry

Being in Ministry

Honestly, Openly, and Deeply

Douglas Purnell

WIPF & STOCK · Eugene, Oregon

BEING IN MINISTRY
Honestly, Openly, and Deeply

Copyright © 2010 Douglas Purnell. All rights reserved. Except for brief quotations in critical publications or reviews, no part of this book may be reproduced in any manner without prior written permission from the publisher. Write: Permissions, Wipf and Stock Publishers, 199 W. 8th Ave., Suite 3, Eugene, OR 97401.

Original woodcut by Chris Wyatt of "Catriona" used with permission of the artist.

Wipf & Stock
An Imprint of Wipf and Stock Publishers
199 W. 8th Ave., Suite 3
Eugene, OR 97401

www.wipfandstock.com

ISBN 13: 978-1-60899-122-8

Manufactured in the U.S.A.

*This book is dedicated to Heather, my wife,
who has been friend and partner in all of the journey.
She has walked the path with me.
She knows.*

Contents

Foreword ix

Acknowledgments xv

Introduction xvii

1. The Journey to the Present Ministry 1
2. Call to Ministry 10
3. Being and Doing in Ministry: Doing 35
4. Privilege 65
5. Being a Theological Interpreter 86
6. Being and Doing in Ministry: Being 113
7. Identity: Memory 137
8. Remembering 144
9. Amen 154
10. Where Am I Now? 159

   Appendix 164

   Bibliography 167

Foreword

ONE OF THE LONELIEST times in ministry occurs in the days, weeks, and even months after a call or appointment has been terminated—especially when it is not expected. The reason makes little difference: a debilitating illness; conflicts with congregation, colleagues, or supervisors, a bishop's decision, an ethical lapse, unresolved tension between institutional and personal expectations, or financial crisis. Emotions associated with unfilled anticipations, severed relationships, and uncertain futures crowd into our consciousness. No matter how rational or objective the reasoning behind the decision, we become sensitive to judgments against us and/or our performance associated with the language of termination, dismissal, redundancy—sometimes even retirement. We find ourselves caught up in self-doubt and confusion, anger, or frustration. We no longer have a place to work or colleagues. We no longer enjoy the institutional confirmation of the calling we have followed or the vocation we have engaged.

For Douglas Purnell, pastoral theologian, theological school professor, and author of this book, a financial crisis in the theological college where he was employed culminated in the elimination of his faculty position. It was rendered "redundant"—deemed superfluous in the midst of resource scarcity. He had not been forewarned of his position's vulnerability. The announcement came as surprise. In the pages that follow he describes the tumultuous ensuing weeks. Feelings of rejection, anger, frustration, and isolation washed over him. Questions, familiar to those in similar circumstances, kept popping into his consciousness:

- Was I deluded to think my calling was central to the mission of this place?
- Was my vocation not valued by my colleagues and supervisors?
- What does it mean to be mentored by church leaders into this ministry only to be dismissed from the position giving that ministry its purpose and form?

- What can I say to colleagues whose jobs were considered more central or valued more highly?
- How do I talk with my family about all that is going on?
- Where am I to go next?
- What am I to be doing?

Yet, as we all soon learn in the midst of some personal or community crisis, the world for Purnell did not stop and wait while he grieved the loss of work and reoriented himself toward something new. Life persists. So Purnell continued to interact—albeit with some awkwardness, with church officials and colleagues. He talked with his family. He worked through the structures of the church for something to do next—eventually accepting a call from a congregation to be its pastor. Perhaps most important, he continued two practices that had been central to his life and ministry—painting and journaling—and give form to these reflections on the recovery of vocation.

Some readers will be drawn to the book for the candor with which Purnell reveals the depths of his response to this experience. They will find words to name their own experience of disrupted calling. Purnell, however, makes a larger contribution. He invites the reader into the rediscovery and revitalization of his calling to ministry through the disciplined and robust exercise of its central practices. In the pages that follow Purnell poignantly and powerfully illustrates how the integrity and rigor of those practices became for him the means to vocational healing. This is not a "pick yourself up by your bootstraps" story, but a candid examination of the recreative power in doing with integrity what one knows.

In this regard *Being in Ministry* complements Heidi Neumark's[1] powerful exploration of call and vocation in the midst of a ministry in a congregation without obvious resources in a neighborhood forgotten by everyone but the people who lived in it and Richard Lischer's[2] evocative story of his journey as a young pastor from seminary into the vitality of an embodied ministry. What distinguishes each of these works is the integrity of their practice—its faithfulness to the transformative possibilities in the vocation of ministry. Even more distinctive is the extent to which they make obvious that it is in the practice of their vocations that they are

---

1. Neumark, *Breathing Space*.
2. Lischer, *Open Secrets*.

sustained, renewed, and energized for living into the demands and challenges of the ministry that centers their vocational self-understanding.

Being in Ministry however, differs in a couple of important ways. The first has to do with the way that Purnell tells his story. He does not weave a seamless narrative based on his reflections of critical moments in his ministry as do Neumark and Lischer. Rather, through a series of vignettes, based primarily on entries from his journal, he invites us into the exercise of what Craig Dykstra has called the pastoral imagination—the way he anticipates, engages, and then reflects back on moments in his ministry. Weddings, funerals, sermons, hospital and home visits—the stuff of daily pastoral practice—become windows through which we might glimpse the shape of his practice and the renewal of his calling. Through his descriptions of these moments in ministry he invites us into a "way of seeing and interpreting" that reveal in Dykstra's words "a kind of internal gyroscope," guiding him "in and through every crevice" of his pastoral work.[3] For Purnell, that "gyroscope" is not something one brings to the practices of ministry. Rather as he writes, it is "forged on the anvil of deep and sustained engagement" with the practices central to the calling to which he has given himself.

Being in Ministry is distinctive in another way. Purnell is an artist with a significant reputation in the art community of Australia. That reputation has been acknowledged in the United States by seminaries that have invited him to spend time on their campuses as artist in residence. Painting is a constant in his life and reflections on the experience of painting interspersed with accounts of ministry throughout the book engage the reader in the exercise of what might be called the interplay of his pastoral and aesthetic imaginations. Just as we are invited into his anticipations of and reflections on his pastoral practice, we are also allowed into the way he anticipates and thinks about what he is doing when he is painting. As he took up his ministry in St. Ives Uniting Church, Purnell's journaling became the daily discipline through which his painting and his ministry cohered into a powerful force—in his case, for vocational healing.

Perspectives, sensibilities, and skills associated with seeing integral to the practice of painting are thereby brought into dialogue with those associated with the listening skills at the heart of pastoral practice. As a

---

3. Dykstra, "Pastoral and Ecclesial Imagination," 41.

pastoral theologian Purnell had given special attention to the practices of listening and conversation in ministry and has written provocatively about the role of listening and conversation in ministry.[4] As an artist he has given similar focused attention to the practices of seeing or observing beyond and beneath the surface of things. He has often said that when he paints he attempts to discern and in turn convey the most basic elements of what he is seeing in a landscape or portrait. The intent is to see what is most really real. Listening has a similar function. In his descriptions of his ministry practice we are given the privilege of engaging the interplay of his seeing and listening into what he perceives to be "most real" about the people he meets; what is "most real" in our stance before God, and what is "most real" about his own relationship to God in the activity of *being* in ministry.

In some ways *Being in Ministry* is a surprise in progress. Purnell accepts a call to be the pastor of a congregation even though he is still hurting and full of self-doubt. He listens with his eyes as much as he sees through his ears, makes judgments about ways of responding in ministry to the particularities of some situation, and reflects upon the appropriateness of that response. In the flow of each moment he discovers resources not only for the ministry situation at hand, but also for some transformation of self and the revitalization of his pastoral calling. In the process he not only models integrity in pastoral practice, he provides clues for negotiating the vicissitudes we experience in that practice.

Many of us in ministry have not been trained to listen with the care that Purnell has been. Even fewer among us are professional artists. Our contexts of ministry pose different challenges from those Purnell faced. Undue attention to these elements in Purnell's story however, misses the point. Rather it has more to do with the integrity of *being* in ministry—the faithfulness embedded in the ways we embrace and engage the practices integral to the calling to which we have given ourselves. In the candor of his descriptions of his own journey of vocational reaffirmation, we can begin to envision possibilities for ourselves when we too must live through the challenges and crises that disrupt the fulfillment of our own vocations. *Being in Ministry* fills a gap in the literature on ministry. It legitimates conversation about difficult and often painful moments in our

---

4. Purnell, *Conversation as Ministry*.

ministries. Perhaps most important, it models possibility for reclaiming and renewing our experiences of disrupted vocation.

Charles R. Foster
Professor of Religion and Education emeritus
Candler School of Theology, Emory University

Acknowledgments

Bringing a book like this to completion is a long and fraught process. Many people contribute along the way. They share their lives, listen to my stories, engage and encourage my thinking, make suggestions, read partly formed manuscripts, see the possibility, and much more. This book could not have come to life without the people who support in this way.

The people of the St. Ives congregation of the Uniting Church in Australia (UCA) in suburban Sydney have welcomed, loved, and trusted me as their minister as I sought to find my way back to pastoral ministry. Pam Walker is the pastoral care worker in the congregation and her interest and support in this book project have kept me alive in ministry. Some of the stories shared in this book involve people from this congregation. At times I have told stories using their names with their permission because I want to acknowledge the integrity of their lived experience.

Mac Nicoll and Peter Barnes read early drafts of the book and saw the possibility.

Terry Trewavas and Norman McDonald have been important and caring friends to my soul in the journey.

Chuck Foster has been an insightful and encouraging conversation partner and his wisdom is reflected in the foreword he has written.

Herbert Anderson, Mark Burrows, and Jaco Hamman are long-time friends with deep connections in theological education who have listened, read, enthused, and encouraged me along the way.

John Oldmeadow and the Board of Education of the UCA in New South Wales gave generous support.

Ulrike Guthrie saw the possibility of a book in bundles of stories and words, has asked the questions that really top-shelf editors ask, and helped me to hone and shape the stories into an engaging and powerful text. She has helped me be patient and persistent. Books take some significant time to find their form.

And Heather has intimately shared the journey.

My gratitude and thanks.

Introduction

We sat at dinner in the home of an artist friend, a huge Central Australian landscape on the wall. One third of the landscape was in darkness. The artist told us that many people criticize his use of darkness in his paintings. They say that they won't be able to hang the work on their walls because the darkness disturbs them. "But," he said, "I can't avoid the darkness." It was as though without darkness the work would not be true to who he is and to how he experiences life. Darkness is part of life.

I agree. And I knew that somehow I had to enter the darkness of my own life. I didn't consciously say "I am going to paint in black," I just found myself doing it. I became attracted to the work of the American abstract expressionist Franz Kline. I looked and looked at his work and wondered, was he influenced by the gradual descent into mental illness and ultimate institutionalization of his wife? I did not try to copy Kline, but I did look at the layering in his work. I looked at the way the black intensified all that was around it. I found that there were red blacks that were more opaque and blue blacks that were more transparent. The blue blacks were, to my eye, the more intense blacks. I wanted to intensify the encounter of the viewer so that they would remember their engagement with this painting. I became enthralled by how an intense black could intensify and bring to life the smallest amount of color.

I hung my paintings around our home to look at them. When my wife began to place large arrangements of hydrangeas in front of them, I realized that she was finding the dark nature of the paintings difficult. We have walked a long way together through life and she knew what had shaped this darkness of mine and how important it was for me to enter into it through my paintings that became a show. She wanted me to find the light and she knew that could not be forced; she just wished that it didn't impinge so heavily on her living space.

Christ Wyatt, another artist friend whose work I describe in this book even now reminds me how significant it was for me to do that work. Chris's wife, Catriona, had recently died and he knew what it was to enter the darkness. The show resonated with this experience of life.

A long time ago when I worked in a psychiatric hospital I learned that people had to enter their own "darkness," be that in the form of a void, wilderness, desert, chaos, nothingness, death, or something similar. When you enter these places with integrity you find life giving images, images that are reflected in the biblical story: order in chaos, water in wilderness, flowers in the desert, resurrection in death, light out of darkness, life-shaping hope.

From theologian Paul Tillich I had learned that some painters paint the way light falls on the surface of things. The images they create are nice, pleasant to look at, reassuring, but they stay on the surface; they do not ask any questions of the viewer. Other artists are more expressive, more emotional; the surface is only surface. The artist has the capacity to push beyond the surface to the depths, to the essence of things, the heart of life itself. These painters seek through their emotional and expressive style to name their own dark places, their deep emotions, their tears, and the hard questions of their own existence.

The dark places are so much a part of life. The surprise, perhaps, is that when with integrity we enter the darkness, we find God hiding there.

That is the journey of this book. I lost a job that I loved, a role that I seemed to have been born for. The hurt and confusion were intense.

Yet to follow Jesus, to honor God, is to walk the way of the cross. There is no promise that in walking that way life will be easy or safe. The task is to find the new direction, the new possibility, the abundant life of which Jesus talks.

This story is about entering the darkness, being alert to the light that comes out from the darkness, and finding the hidden God.

Forty years after being ordained, I'm into my third year in ministry in the St. Ives parish of the Uniting Church, in Sydney, Australia. It has been quite a journey, and most recently a perplexing one that has made me question my calling. St. Ives is a suburban Sydney church. The suburb developed in the late 1960s and early '70s. Many of the people who make up the St. Ives congregation came to the suburb back then and their careers developed so that they became managers and leaders. As their children grew, a large, cohesive, life-shaping group of youth and young adults attended the church. These young people have long since moved on to marriage and work and other places, shaping their own lives. Much of the forty-year-old housing is being bulldozed and replaced by medium density housing, and people who have retired and downsized are currently moving in.

For more than twenty years, the St. Ives church has offered to the wider community divorce and grief recovery groups for people who have lived through these life-shattering events. Over a thousand people have had their lives transformed through participation in these groups. Sadly, the programs are coming to an end now, and the church has had to find a new identity and a new sense of mission.

The church building is a wonderful gift. Built in the 1970s as a flexible seven-day-a-week church, it is solid, substantial, and sacred. It is also in constant use.

The worship space has a sanctuary that is both bright and light. It can be closed off to become a chapel seating up to ninety people. The main body of the church is open and versatile. The chairs are stacked away after worship and the space used for many other activities during the week. It is a great space in which to lead worship. The natural light connects us to land and nature in a way deeply characteristic of Australian spirituality.

I greatly enjoy working with this community. Having been managers, the people are willing to "do" and are not so interested in holding meetings. People offer to take on particular roles, and they justify the trust they are given by getting on with their tasks. They like quality worship, they want to be informed about faith and life, and they think hard about who they are as a people of faith. Any public presentation has to be done professionally just as any task an individual or group takes on is done to the highest standards.

Being in ministry in this congregation at this stage of my life is a gift to me. I am in my sixties, and as far as I can currently see, this will be my last parish. This is the fourth parish in which I have been minister in the forty years since ordination. As part of my ministry I also spent ten years teaching pastoral theology in a seminary. Although my energy and that of my largely aging congregation is waning, we continue to do new and exciting things. A couple of years ago we began a "tradition" of inviting fifteen leading Australian artists to produce a contemporary visual image representing a Station of the Cross for a special Easter exhibition each year. That has been so well received that this year we are adding to it: we have asked fifteen emerging composers to create a new piece of music for us for a concert reflecting the Stations of Creation to be held in Advent. We want to offer the wider community deep experiences of Easter and of Christmas. There is an excitement that together we are doing new things.

My journey to be minister of St. Ives parish was not easy for me and their journey to have me as minister was not easy for them. I had been teaching in theological education for ten years when my position in pastoral theology was made redundant and I with it. On the part of the parish, the previous St. Ives minister resigned after just four months in the parish. A hurting and uncertain community and a hurting and uncertain minister were pushed together and we have gradually found our way forward to new life and new ministry.

This book tells some of that story, not out of a desire to vent the pain (which at times felt insurmountable) but out of the struggle to find a new direction, a new sense of call in ministry when a previous call that seemed so loud, so strong, and so affirmed had been abruptly pulled away. Yet it is also more than that: after ten years of teaching pastoral theology I wanted to reflect publicly and theologically on pastoral practice. I wanted to do what I had been teaching. I had become aware that many in ministry had lost confidence in their role as pastoral leaders; they were not sure what priestly presence might mean, how it might be valued, or how it might be lived. So I set out to describe what I was doing in ministry as a way of reflecting on the tasks of ministry.

The stories[5] that follow all in some way reflect on what it means for me both to *be* a priestly person and what I *do* as a priestly person, day to day.

But I am not only a priestly person, I am also a professional artist. When I paint, I put out an image and I want people to respond to the painting in light of their own stories and experience rather than my having to explain my intention in the painting. Likewise, in this book I tell lots of stories about myself as minister and artist, but I want the stories to speak for themselves, and to break open your stories, too, your experience and reflection. I hope that the stories will help you to discern the light that comes out from the darkness in your experience.

I have sought to write in a way that reflects my commitment to living honestly, openly, and deeply as a spiritual leader. This means that I do not have answers to all the things that happen in my life or the lives of those in my care. It means that I am always attempting to live with the uncertainty and vulnerability of going into the rocky wilderness places of others. And it means that my writing and painting are ways of acknowledging the mystery that lies beyond where our normal speech will reach. Here, the sacred symbols that we share help us name God and the times of darkness and despair and the moments of light and exhilaration in our lives, and that is why we continue to break bread together, drink wine together, be together, and bless one another.

Whether as a priest or a layperson, in the ordinary experiences of life, we are not alone. It requires courage to "be" in the face of existential anxiety, and a priestly person more than most others is required to enter life's toughest places with the people given to his or her care. In these tough places the priestly person discerns and mediates in some way the blessing of God. Since the priestly person spends every day and a lifetime

---

5. The stories can be told in the way they are because for almost the entire forty years of my ministry I have written a daily journal reflecting on my practice of ministry and the other things going on in my life. It has been part of my prayer discipline. In the early years of ministry I wanted to be listened to with the same discipline that I had been taught/had learned to listen to others. The simplest answer at the time was to begin writing about what was happening to me each day and then asking the questions of myself that I might ask of others. I learned over time the importance of objective observation and description even though I might be a subjective participant. I wrote then about my feelings and emotions in relation to what had happened and I attempted to listen for the emerging questions and to make appropriate connections with the tradition of faith, with other writers and thinkers and artists, and so on. The discipline of daily journaling is implicit as a key part of the discipline that enables this book to find the form that it does.

entering into such tough places and is called on again and again to convey God's presence and blessing in precisely such tough places, I hope the stories—and images—that follow will remind you how to keep on doing that, life long.

In particular, I have wanted to share through this text the disciplines involved in being present to the lived experience of the other, to the received Christian tradition, and to the imaginative actions that enable people to discern the voice of God breaking into life in fresh ways. Being always both artist and priest, these stories from my life are the best way I know to break open in gentle ways the darkness that so often settles upon us. It is also the best way I know to break open the layers of questions, ideas, and possibilities about what we are and what we do as priests, and particularly how we might continue to understand our call throughout our changing lives.

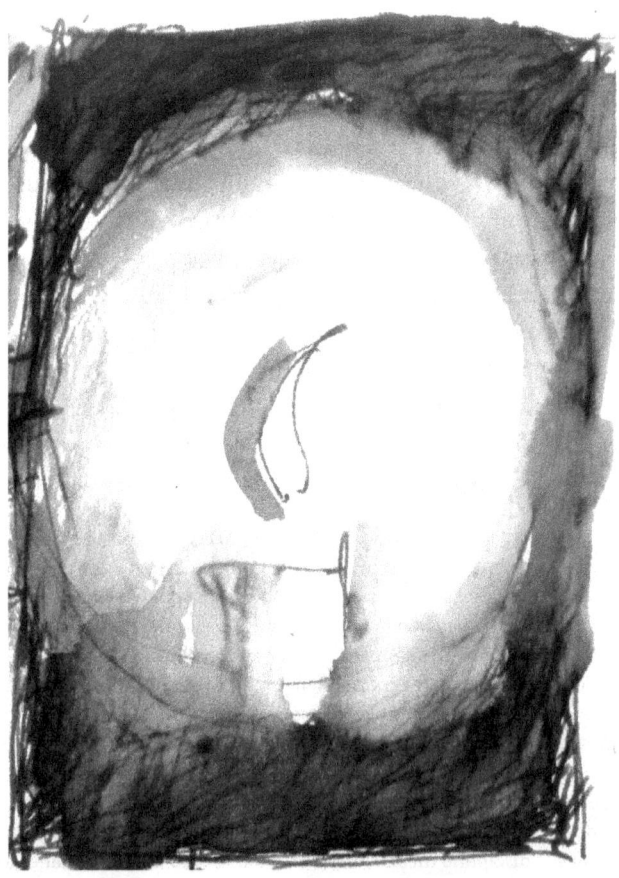

1

The Journey to the Present Ministry

PEOPLE OFTEN ASK ME, "How did you get to *be* a minister?" And so the first part of this book tells the story of that being and of that call, my call—for the particulars are different for every person.

A second question often follows: "As a minister, what do you *do*, day by day?" Or, to put it another way, "What does your work involve?" And so the second part of this book tells about doing in ministry. But it also tells about being. Though we often forget that aspect of our spiritual and priestly lives, or don't trust it enough, in fact being is often all we can do.

Then there is often a third question: about how I became an artist, closely followed by a fourth, whether I'm still painting. Much as folks ask whether my father was a minister, they ask, "Was there an artist in the family in an earlier generation?" No, I say, my dad was a life insurance salesman. As for the question of whether I'm still painting, I always want to answer: "Am I still breathing?" Painting is something that is similar to breathing for me: I do it because I've got to do it. Perhaps you have something in your life that is similarly integral to who you are. You will understand that there are many parallels between my being an artist and my being a priestly person and spiritual leader. And as you find your way through this book, you will see that it is pulsing with drawings and paintings and stories that, while primarily about who I am as artist, are also significantly about who I am as minister, pastor, priestly person, and spiritual leader.

I tell these stories about my own life as a way of making sense of my call, my sense of vocation, and of discerning new directions in the face of major disruption. The stories are also a way of doing pastoral theology— the art and discipline of tending and attending to the lived experience of the people given to my care and holding that experience in conversation with the received church tradition in order to try to make sense of it, or at least to bear it.

I wonder how my stories will prompt you to recall stories about your own life. I particularly hope that the book will encourage you to embrace with confidence and a good measure of relief what your life calls out in you, perhaps as a spiritual leader, minister, and priestly person, but perhaps as something different altogether.

Since many of us have experienced similar painful disruptions in our lives, I have included stories that I hope will evoke your memory and your story. At the conclusion of the book in an appendix is a series of reflective questions that I hope will help you reflect on your own life and ministry

The stories I tell are not all easy or straightforward. My position as a teacher in a seminary was made redundant and the strong sense of call I had was ripped apart causing what for me was a vocational and life crisis. I was suddenly enveloped by darkness. Subsequently I have had to rethink my life and ministry. I know that I am not alone in this, for many of you have faced similar crises that have pulled apart, unsettled, and radically challenged the sense of call or vocation that was shaping what you were doing.

PRIVILEGE

I like being in ministry. It is a privilege. Being in ministry is what my life calls out in me. That sense of call has been present from an early age, and through the last three years when the actions of the church by making my position as a seminary teacher redundant have hurt and confused me, that sense of call to ministry has remained clear.

A colleague minister asked me one day, "Have you thought of doing something else, outside the church?" "No," I said, "I am a priestly person. That is what my life calls out in me; that is what I am. I have thought about doing other things, but I have never had any sense that they would be in the least bit satisfying. I am a minister, a pastoral person, a spiritual leader."

Yet in 2004, after I had taught for nine years in a seminary, I was abruptly beckoned from a meeting and told that because of a financial crisis in the institution they had decided to cut two teaching positions. Mine was one. Somehow I held myself together until I got home and told Heather, my wife; then, I broke down and wept uncontrollably. I was devastated. Teaching had been such a clear and affirmed call. Never until this moment had there been any doubt for me that this was "my calling" in life. Now here I was: made redundant, downsized.

MY CALL TO THEOLOGICAL EDUCATION

My call to theological education happened slowly over about fifteen years. I had responded to the call to ministry and had understood pastoral ministry as being the direction of my life. Slowly a new sense of call emerged within that larger call; it was to teach in seminary. One of the more consciously shaping moments happened like this: while I was on a sabbatical from my parish in Sydney, Australia, I was invited to teach a weeklong course at San Francisco Theological Seminary in art and theology. At the end of the final class, I thanked the students, picked up my things, and began to leave the room. One of the students stood on behalf of the class and presented me with a preaching stole. Apparently I had been seen covetously eyeing that particular stole in the seminary bookshop—and had decided I could not afford it. The student's words of presentation were very complimentary about the learning experience we had shared and strongly affirmed my call to a teaching ministry. The gift came as a clear blessing of the call that had been growing in momentum for a very long time.

I had not been a very good undergraduate student. I didn't do exams at all well. In retrospect, I suspect that I was asking too many questions, enjoying learning new things, playing with ideas, but not able to ground them in any significant way.

I found a way that suited my learning style when I was introduced to a process of learning by reflecting on experience. I began to shape and address my own questions. My learning had a newfound direction.

That learning style was reinforced when a church resource person came to our local congregation to lead a program on Lay Evangelism. Instead of telling us what to do, he asked about our experience and got us telling stories about our lives. Suddenly I was empowered to learn in a different way. I asked that leader where he had learned to do this and with his guidance found opportunities to practice such inductive learning skills. I put a great deal of energy into learning how groups functioned and into training and working as a group leader. When I understood that families were also small groups that could benefit from this style of collaborative leadership, I trained as a Family Therapist. The whole idea of learning by reflecting on lived experience made sense to me and gave me new purpose and direction as a human being, minister, priestly person, and as a marriage partner and parent.

One sunny afternoon I was standing on a street corner in Melbourne, talking to a colleague in ministry. He was someone I admired, someone a couple of years older than me. He told me there was a position in theological education coming available at the seminary and suggested that I apply. I was a bit staggered, because I had never imagined myself in that sort of role. I had been in pastoral ministry at this stage for ten years; four of those years had been in an outer suburban new area ministry and the other years in an intense inner city mission. It would be another fifteen years before I became a full-time seminary teacher.

Not too much later, I met and found a ready rapport with Sandra Brown, a Princeton seminary professor on sabbatical in Australia. She participated in groups that I ran and encouraged me to consider going to Princeton for a time as a visiting scholar. I was fortunate to be awarded a fellowship that helped me get there. Sandra invited me to teach in her class at Princeton; hers was one of the many loud voices that directed me towards becoming a theological educator.

On my return to Australia, I noticed an advertisement in a church paper for an "innovative teacher of Pastoral Theology" at United Theological College in Sydney. That seemed my thing. And by this time I was being encouraged by many people to consider becoming a seminary teacher. So when I saw this particular advertisement, I called the principal of the Theological College in Sydney; though he told me that the position had already been filled, he encouraged me to prepare myself further by doing some extra study.

Graeme Griffin was professor of pastoral theology when I went to Theological School in Melbourne. Graeme had introduced me to Sandra Brown and had invited me on a number of occasions to teach in his classes. When I moved from Melbourne to Sydney to take up a new parish, Graeme came to me saying, "I'm disappointed that you are moving to Sydney because I had hoped that you would be able to take up a more significant teaching role with me." And when I arrived in Sydney I found that he had written a letter of strong commendation of me as teacher in the field of pastoral theology to the then principal of the Theological College in Sydney.

Soon after I arrived in Sydney, I was invited to become part of the pastoral theology "team" at United Theological College. The college had decided that their "innovative way of teaching" pastoral theology was to have a team of four people. I was made an adjunct faculty person and invited to share in all the things that the faculty did. The other faculty members encouraged me in every way they could to study and to contribute in theological education.

One afternoon the principal of the college asked to see me. He said there were a number of positions that would soon become available in theological education, and advised, "You ought to begin doctoral studies in order that you can be ready when they become available." So with the encouragement of the principal, I completed a doctorate as suggested. During this time I continued to be a parish minister and to teach in the Theological College.

When in 1994 I took my long-service sabbatical from the parish, I went to be an artist in residence at Wesley Theological Seminary in Washington, D.C. This placed me full time within a seminary for a number of months. I was delighted, first, in being an artist and contributing to the community in that way, and second, in being in conversation with theological scholars, especially those in the field of pastoral theology. I was enormously stimulated by my experiences there.

One weekend I went out to visit a friend at the seminary of which he was president. David had been on sabbatical in Sydney a year or so earlier. He greeted me by telling me he had just had a phone call from the people at the seminary in Sydney asking for his advice about the appointment of a new principal. Looking straight at me, David said: "I told them to appoint you."

To say my head spun would be an understatement. I spent the train trip back to Washington, D.C. imagining what I would do if I were principal of such an institution. When I returned to Sydney I consulted people about whether this was an appropriate thing for me and wisely, at the time, people told me it wasn't.

About the same time a half-time position in pastoral theology was advertised at the seminary. A friend and colleague whose advice I have always valued told me that I should apply for this position. It seemed crazy because I had three teenage children, and working half time did not seem a reasonable thing to do. He was persuasively adamant that I would find a way to make the other half of my income. Fortunately a full-time position became available almost immediately. With much encouragement from many people, I applied for and was offered the position. It was what my life had called out in me.

The people of the parish where I was ministering understood the strength of the call to theological education and were supportive in my transition from parish to theological college. I had been in pastoral ministry for twenty-five years in three quite different parishes in three states and would take that rich experience to the seminary.

My friend and fellow minister, Brian Howe, who had just resigned as Deputy Prime Minister of the country, agreed to preach at my induction. His willingness to do so was another of the many affirmations of my call. As he spoke on that day, I thought, "If I can help equip other people to contribute to society as you have, I will have done my job." For the induction service, I wore the stole given me by the students at SFTS. Their words of presentation remain with me.

I seemed to have found the place to which my life was calling me. I loved teaching. And I enjoyed reflecting and writing on the educational processes and how they contributed to transformational learning. I wrote about experiential learning processes in the classroom, about using creative projects as an integrative way of doing assessment tasks, and about the imagination in theological education, about being a "body."

I taught my students to shape and answer their own learning questions, to be "self-evaluating" for I had learned in ministry that not relying on others' evaluation was important. So, I expected my students to set out their learning goals, to write out their learning strategies, and then, at the end of the course, not only to identify how well they thought they had done in the course but also to give themselves a grade. I read their work as well, gave it a grade, and then we put the two side by side and averaged them. Most of the time the grades were actually very close, and when they weren't we had to talk.

I wanted students to practice intentional conversations that they would have when they were in ministry and so encouraged them to do that. I linked art and theology as a way of addressing the imagination of the students and of helping them to integrate their thinking. Mainly I did it and do it to stay alive to how God's voice might break fresh into the world through the great acts of the imagination within our particular culture.

I spent my sabbaticals as an artist and scholar in residence in Washington and Boston, and visited seminaries in Tonga, the Philippines, England, and the United States to sit in on classes and to see how other teachers taught. In 2003 I published a book entitled *Conversation as*

Ministry, and whenever possible I gave an account of my teaching and my scholarship by presenting papers at conferences around the world.

On top of my normal teaching load the principal asked me to take on the role of being course coordinator for a new Doctor of Ministry program, one way in which professional education offers an opportunity for mid-life, mid-career reflection on practice. It seems to me that a quality doctorate depends on the quality of the supervision and so I jumped at the chance to train supervisors to offer the best supervision they could for such action-reflection degrees.

I loved teaching and I loved the academic environment. My teaching was affirmed by my colleagues, by the number of students taking my courses, by student evaluations, and by the work I was having published. My peers in the field of pastoral theology both within Australia and overseas acknowledged the significance of what I was doing. The principal of the college told me I was a valued member of the team. These things all seemed to reinforce my sense of the appropriateness of my call to be in theological education.

So you will understand that when I was beckoned from a meeting and told that the seminary council had voted to make the position of lecturer in pastoral theology redundant, I was devastated. It remains hard to comprehend what happened and how it happened, particularly when my call to theological education had seemed so clear and so fitting. My devastation increased as the wider church hesitated to address an appeal about the justice of the decision. Some months later a Committee of Appeal determined that the process of making the position redundant was flawed in that there had been inadequate consultation and that "a serious injustice had been done. A written and a published apology should be made." Yet there seemed little willingness or capacity to either make the apology or to publicly acknowledge the grief the decision had caused. I wanted and needed some public recognition of my contribution to the church in theological education and that didn't come. Such recognition would have made it easier to move on. I felt as if I was the victim of bad process and bad decision-making and that I was being persecuted for being that victim. It was an awful time for me and I guess for many others.

When my denomination's Synod then invited me to be in conversation with the parish of St. Ives about becoming their pastor, you can imagine I was very uncertain about how to move ahead, particularly without the same clear sense of call I had felt to theological education.

THE END OF A CALL

Up until the moment when my theological education position was made redundant, I had never had any doubt that the best gift that I had to offer the church in ministry was as a seminary teacher. It was the strangest and most difficult of times. For at the same time as I was told that my services as a professor were no longer required, I received a tremendously affirming performance review. As time went on, people in the church made many promises about my future as a teacher that they didn't keep. I found that very difficult. I lost trust in people, and I lost confidence in the church I had loved.

I was hurt, confused, and scared. I knew clearly that I was called to ministry. Yet the task that I had thought I would work on until retirement had been taken away from me. I had to find a new direction.

I was wary of returning to parish or pastoral ministry. It didn't seem the best use of my gifts for the church, and besides I wasn't convinced I had the energy to do parish work again. Certainly, I didn't have the naive energy that I had had when I was younger.

Besides, I had become used to sitting with my wife in worship in the local church. I had become used to having weekends off. And though I admired the way that Geoff, the local minister, gave himself to a diverse community and was able to let them all have a voice in such a way that the church was truly inclusive and growing, I wasn't at all sure that I could do that. Moreover, Heather and I had bought our own home when I moved into theological education, a home that was convenient to her work, and

one where she had created a nourishing garden. She did not want to move house for my job. (I have never moved house for Heather's job in our thirty-five years of marriage.) Heather liked worshipping in the local community, she had a spiritual home, and she did not want to become the "minister's spouse" in a new congregation. Since I liked being married to Heather and wanted to continue being married to her, her needs were an important part of my decision-making process.

Eventually and reluctantly (because it meant acknowledging that my academic life was over), I accepted a call to be minister of the Uniting Church parish of St. Ives in northern Sydney. Certainly I imagined that my twenty-five years of parish experience and ten years in theological education, along with my writings and reflection, would stand me in good stead for this new parish ministry to which I was being called, and that I would find a way to do it well, even if I began it with anxiety.

As I began this new ministry, I found myself writing reflectively about the things I was doing, spurred on by a comment by a reader of my earlier book that it allowed him the sense of looking over the shoulder of an experienced pastor as he engaged in pastoral conversation. Could I write as openly and vulnerably about who I am and what I do as a minister and artist as I had about pastoral conversation? Could I express what it is to be a priestly person, a communicator of liminality, one comfortable with life and death and mystery?

In writing the stories gathered in these pages, I have become increasingly aware that to "be" in ministry—just as to be an artist—requires disciplined reflection and a continual rewriting of the story of one's life as almost every encounter with a person, event, image, and idea is an occasion to rethink one's identity as a (pastoral and priestly) person.

Three years down the track, I rejoice that there is life for me in ministry, beyond the academy. I am reminded of a ministerial colleague who turned down a full-time teaching opportunity because, as he said, he didn't want to give up the privilege of blessing the people at the close of worship each week. Indeed, pastoral ministry offers me opportunities to be invited into the intimate spaces of people's lives and blessing them. It is an extraordinary privilege.

This, then, is the story of how I pushed into the darkness and wrestled with my calling, of how I reconfigured my understanding of what that calling is for me and what being in ministry entails. This is the story of how I came to be aware of the light that comes out of darkness.

2

Call to Ministry

RETURN TO PARISH MINISTRY

Just as I seek to live honestly, openly, deeply, and humbly as a spiritual leader, so too do I strive to *be* in this book. My choice to be vulnerable in this way is because I think people's uncertainty in ministry has led to a lack of confidence and an increased privacy among spiritual leaders about their life and being, neither of which seems particularly helpful or fitting. It certainly wasn't helpful to me as I wrestled with redundancy and calling.

LIFE AS AN ARTIST: WHAT I DO AS AN ARTIST

In the interests of honesty, openness, and living truthfully and deeply, I need to tell you about the other part of my life and calling, a part that is not overtly ministry, though I'd argue the similarities and practices are striking. I am an artist.

> *I am an artist"* [said Vincent,] *"— . . . the word of course includes the meaning: always seeking without absolutely finding. It is just the converse of saying 'I know I have found it.' As far as I know the word means: 'I am seeking, I am striving, I am in it with all of my heart.'"*[1]

I have a long discipline as an artist. I began to paint in my twenties, and for more than thirty years I have drawn and painted with discipline. I carry a sketchbook wherever I go. I draw every day. Every week I go to a life drawing group where I draw the human figure for two hours. I go into my studio every day and look at the work in progress. I buy and read monographs on artists so that I can develop a keen sense of what other artists have done. I visit art galleries as often as I can simply to look and learn from how others have done it. I share a regular lunch with other artists where we talk about and critique each other's work. I work hard to make paintings. A lovely quotation by Rainer Maria Rilke on my studio wall reminds me to keep the whole process in perspective, to help me slow down and be patient. It is above where I put my canvases when I am painting so that I can see and digest it easily. As secretary to the great sculptor, Auguste Rodin, Rilke wrote, "One day, I was walking through that vast studio and I saw that everything was in the process of becoming and nothing was in a hurry."

From Rilke I have learned that I must go into the studio and look, become familiar with my own work, listen hard, and allow it to address me slowly in its own time and way. I need to remember that "everything is in the process of becoming, and nothing is in a hurry." Then I paint, and I paint, and I paint. I know that if I continue to put marks on the canvases that eventually some good paintings will emerge. The process requires a courageous commitment to paint over what I have already created in the hope that I can create something new. Picasso said: "[D]estroy one's picture, recreate it many times. On each destruction of a beautiful find,

---

1. Roskill, *Letters*, 148.

the artist does not suppress it, to tell the truth; rather he transforms it, condenses it, makes it more substantial."[2]

It is as important to me to paint as it is to breathe. It is what I do.

Being an artist is an expression of my soul. Being an artist is not about having an odd personality, or wearing a black beret, or sitting in cafes all day long, or talking about making art. Being an artist involves looking at the world with discipline, being present to life in all its forms, knowing and loving the materials that I use, and having a drivenness to express a response to my being in this world that is somewhere beyond speech. It involves strength of personal identity, a capacity to live with uncertainty, and the courage to place one's ego literally on the wall, and then to be open to the critique of others.

Soon after I began ministry in St. Ives Parish I discovered the delight of their "Special Events," especially their "trad" jazz concerts. Two or three times a year a traditional or big band jazz concert is held in the church on a Saturday night. Typically three hundred people come.

With my sketchbook and pen and water brush in hand, I find a seat close to the front and I do what I love doing: I draw the musicians in full flight. The music excites my drawing. I make marks on the page, all the time becoming more frenetic as the music gains in pace and energy. Some of these drawings you'll see in this book.

My hope is that you will be able to "cut loose" with these stories as a good swing player does with music, and take them where you need or want to go.

2. From a conversation between Christian Zervos and Pablo Picasso included in Ghiselin, *Creative Process*, 50.

WRITING AS A PASTORAL THEOLOGIAN

I write as a pastoral theologian, one who thinks about people being formed and transformed in the tradition and practices of the Christian faith; one who attends with discipline to the lived experience of the other, whether individual, couple, family, group, or society; and one who holds lived experience in conversation with the received tradition in such a way that I can respond both by praising God and by practicing care and justice. In order to function in this way as a pastoral leader, I need to know myself as an individual, family, spiritual, and cultural person, practice the art of attending or paying attention, I need to be able to imagine the conversations that come when lived experience is held in conversation with the tradition, and then to know how to be and do that which brings care and justice. Like making music and like painting, such pastoral practices are acts of the imagination.

WHAT DO YOU DO?

I called in on an artist friend one afternoon, and he asked me, "What do you do as a pastor?"

So I described what I do with my time each day. "I visit and talk with the people, I prepare for worship. I visit the people in hospital when they are sick, I conduct funerals...." It occurred to me that there was a lot that I didn't and perhaps couldn't say. For example, would it sound pretentious to say, "I seek to be present to people when they encounter the tougher questions of their living. I seek to be there when they wonder about life." It wasn't adequate then and it doesn't seem adequate now. And yet it is true.

Besides, I've got to confess I felt a bit as if I were being asked to justify what I do as being "work." And yet this particular friend would have understood those dimensions of my work that could not have been quantified or described as outcomes. He understands that society needs spiritual leaders just as it needs artists and musicians.

Then I realized that it was harder still to convey (and to have someone accept) that much of my job or task or calling is about what I am—about my being rather than my doing.

Many years ago, I led a team of pastors into a community that had been devastated by fire. We walked among the ruins engaging whoever we could find in conversation; seeking to get them to talk about their experience, listening to their shock, supporting in whatever ways we could. The day was difficult: Had I contributed anything of worth?

At the end of the day I came across a young man filling the large water tank on the back of his truck. Being envious of the clarity of his task for him, I commented on how he knew what he had to do, whereas I felt very uncertain, just walking around talking to people. His response as he closed the cab door on his water truck and drove away—"We all have our jobs to do"— has stayed with me. Yes, we all have our jobs to do.

For some reason we are intrigued by how a person becomes a minister or an artist or a circus clown more so than how a person becomes a banker, teacher, or merchant seaman. Is it because the career track is less obvious? Or the job more mysterious and liminal? Perhaps the difference is just this: that ministry is about being and not just doing, and the former is much harder to grasp. This book tells stories that break open what it is to be.

I HEARD A VOICE

So how did I become a minister? One reads about it happening this way, but it is true: I had in fact heard a "voice" call me to ministry as a ten-year-old boy. It didn't make sense then, and it barely makes sense now. We were living on a dairy farm at the time. I was walking down the back path towards the dairy. I heard a voice from somewhere, seemingly coming out of a tree behind me, say: "I want you to be a minister."

My life was calling out something in me, and over time my local church and the wider church agreed about it, and educated me for and then ordained me to the "ministry of the word."

Call to ministry is complex and shaped by many things: the mysterious and mystical sense of call (experienced in so many different ways), personal identity shaped both by genetics and nurture, transforming experiences, the prayers of others, the encouragement of mentors, and the confirmation of the church. Call is both about the whole of my life, who I am as a human being, and it is particularly about what role in ministry I have within the church.

THE BEGINNING OF A CALL

We lived on a remote farm in Australia, five miles from the closest town with its general store, butcher, baker, pub, and a couple of churches. The "big" town with ten thousand people was a further fifteen miles away. I went to a one-teacher primary school with thirty students aged between five and twelve. We got a ride to school in the back of the milk truck if we were ready on time in the morning, and walked the mile and a half home in the afternoon. At home there were chores: filling the wood box, getting the cows in, helping with the milking.

School and home each had their part in forming me. The Alfred Lawrence Sexton memorial prize I won two years in a row for good citizenship seemed to foretell the life I would live. The plaque somberly parsed:

Alfred	Good Counselor	the scroll
Laurence	Crowned with the laurel	the wreath
Sexton	Variant of Sacristan, one who cares for sacred things	hence the staff of office and garb

> The sacristan has laid down Alfred's scroll and his own staff of office to hold open the door of school or church or place of "Good Counsel" and offer the torch of Life and Wisdom for the Way to those who go forth to win the Laurel."

The "good counselor who cares for things sacred, who holds open the doors of faith and learning in order that people might find life and wisdom" describes something of the ministry into which I have lived.

My preparation for such lofty achievements at school began at home, of course, though not in the predictable way perhaps. My mum had died when I was seven. Her name was Elsie and I talk of her as my birth mother. My dad remarried and my three siblings and I had moved to "the farm," I later learned, so that we would have the space to make relationships with our new mother, Elizabeth, without there being people around who had known our birth mother. Thinking about that decision fifty years on, it seemed a good one.

Sundays we would go into the local town to go to church. Dad dropped us children off at the Anglican Church in the hope that there might be someone to teach us Sunday School, while my second mother went to Catholic Mass, and Dad waited for us, reading the Sunday papers. We often walked past the milk factory on our way to meet our parents at the general store after church. If we were lucky we were given a pint of milk, before going on to buy an ice cream—the weekly treat.

It was on one such Sunday afternoon when I was wandering down the back path towards the dairy in my own dream world that I heard the voice announcing, "I want you to be a minister," brought me up with a jolt. I was no more than ten years old and I didn't know any ministers. The memory of that voice is so intense, that I can still hear it today.

There is nothing rational or logical about the voice. I become silent when I think about it. It is a strange moment in my mind that has shaped the whole of my life.

Not long afterwards we moved from the farm. My father stopped taking us to church. He told me that was the only time our maternal grandmother expressed concern about how we children were being parented. She insisted we needed to be taken to church, and he took us. Later, we moved to the big city and Dad found a church that would be a good "home" for me. He came to church with me regularly until finally I left home for theological college (seminary), after which he became a Catholic because he thought that a husband and wife ought to worship together.

The voice, the sentence I heard on that afternoon, has shaped the path of my life. At the end of school I applied for some jobs, and I became a candidate for ministry within the Presbyterian Church of Australia, which in 1977 became part of the Uniting Church in Australia. The local church talked with me about my sense of call, and the presbytery and the principal of the theological college all listened and then confirmed the sense that the voice had called out in me. The church sent me to university and then theological college, and after six years of tertiary study, ordained me.

I was unclear then about what ministry was really about. I had studied Bible and theology and pastoral care. But once in the parish I had to become a spiritual leader. I had to lead the people in worship, to help shape mission, to visit the people, to try to plant a new church and run two older ones, and in between I had to teach scripture in schools, conduct on average one funeral every week, and run a youth group in a new area development with up to ninety kids converging on our home because there were no facilities in the community—all that in addition to finishing my university studies and getting used to being a husband and father.

I didn't do it very well. Nearly forty years have passed since my ordination, many more since I heard that voice calling me. I have ministered in three very different parishes, taught in theological education for ten years, and have now returned to parish ministry.

I am continually reviewing my identity as a minister, a priestly person, and a spiritual leader. I'm continually rethinking the stories that shape my identity and asking myself questions like, Who prayed for your ordination? And, how do I identify, respect, and honor the light that comes out from the darkness?

THE SHAPING OF MY DAD'S PRAYER

Though I have the sense that my birth mum, my grandmother, and my second mother prayed for my ordination, it is of my dad's prayer, shaped in the years before I was born, that I am most acutely aware.

As a young child I had seen the family photos of my dad in his air force uniform, sergeant's stripes on his shoulders, standing proudly in front of a Lancaster bomber. In my child's mind, that image of him reflected, first, that my dad had contributed significantly to the Allies winning the war, and, second, that my father was committed to the violence of war. That childhood interpretation shaped political and social decisions that I made in subsequent years. In time and with more information I came to choose for myself quite different values.

There came a time when I needed to know a lot more about my life from my father. I needed to know about his life and I needed to know about the illness and death of my mother when I was seven years old. Getting these stories would, I thought, help me live more appropriately in my marriage and help me to know my identity and to live the ministry to which I was called.

The story as I tell it here is my story; it is the way I heard it, the way I remembered it, the way I have told it, and the way it has shaped my being as marriage partner, as father, as artist, and as a spiritual leader and priestly person.

The process of asking my dad to tell me about his life began with a few questions I asked when I was thirty. Those questions began a conversation I continued with him until the time of his death more than twenty years later.

I would have known that the story wasn't straightforward had I reflected on the rules that existed in my family. One very strong rule was that we were never allowed to have toy guns in our home, nor were we allowed to point our finger at someone as though it were a pretend gun. I remember my inner turmoil when an uncle brought to our home a bundle of water pistols that he had purchased. It was a scorching hot day and he had a great sense of play. We had been given these "guns" and were of course expected to point them and fire the water in them at each other, as a game. I was uncertain as to how my father would have responded and inside I anguished, not wanting to offend him. I need not have worried: he joined the game for the fun that it was.

As a young boy, just after the end of World War II, occasionally I said things that were anti-German or anti-Japanese, and my dad would quickly tell me that all people were capable of doing such things. He told of his distress at seeing American soldiers make a German prisoner hold his arms above his head, and every time they fell below his shoulders they hit him in the ribs with a baseball bat. It was difficult as an eight- or nine-year-old to understand where those stories came from because they were part of Dad's experience from before I was born.

I discovered that my paternal grandfather had been critically injured in World War I while my father was a toddler at home. He was permanently incapacitated and needed a great deal of care from his wife and his only son—my dad. He died when my father was eighteen. Rather than my father being an advocate of war, I found that he had been an active conscientious objector to Australia's involvement in a war in Europe. He spoke before groups of people about his objections to participation in a war in Europe.

Yet one day he told me that when the Japanese attacked Sydney Harbor, he had "stood transfixed, in Martin Place" (the downtown part of the city) and felt it his duty to enlist to defend his country. Why did he not opt to serve in the ambulance division, or in a noncombative role, I wondered. His terse reply: "Once you are in the machine you are in the machine."

So, my father became part of the air force. He did a significant part of his training in Vancouver, Canada, and then went to the UK where he flew bombing and leafleting raids from England over Germany. I have since found out that the life expectancy for people flying those raids was just six weeks.

My dad flew only two missions in his five days with squadron 626 before his plane was shot down and he had to parachute out. On the ground he was picked up and was being passed out of the country through the Underground movement when he was taken prisoner and was interrogated in the San Gilles prison in Brussels. One of the strongest values for my father was to tell the truth, not to lie. So, not wanting to betray his friends, when he was asked by the German officers to name his flight crew, he refused to name them, giving only his name, rank, and serial number, which was all that was required of him. He was placed in a cell and deprived of food. Meals were placed outside of the door of his cell so that he could smell them. Eventually the German officer said to him, "You have a job to do and we have a job to do. Just make up some names." My dad said, "You will know, and I will know that I am telling a lie, but OK, I was flying with (here he listed the names of a number of Australian Bushrangers) Ned Kelly, Ben Hall, Dan Morgan . . ." At which the German officer said, "It is an offense punishable by death to tell a lie to a German officer. Take him out and shoot him!"

But once outside they lifted a trapdoor in the ground and put him in a dungeon. There he remained for seven days, accompanied by rats and disoriented by permanently lit lights. He told with some warmth of the German officer who sat guarding the dungeon reading his Bible, and how when he lifted the trap door the light would come flooding in. That officer allowed my dad to walk outside for hours at a time, so long as he was carrying his toilet bucket. That story has always been important to me; it seemed to name in a very clear way that when my dad was in one of the darkest places in his life, the light flooded into the darkness. It is a story of hope from my family that resonates with the story of faith and the things that I believe.

Later, in the brutal northern winter of 1945, my father had spent about eighteen months in prison before the Russians attacked the Germans from the north, forcing them to retreat with ten thousand prisoners of war, among them my father. These prisoners had not been well fed, were not physically fit, nor equipped with appropriate clothing for the march that followed in the coldest northern winter for many years. Some of them walked eight hundred kilometers, or five hundred miles, over the next few months. If they fell behind or collapsed on the side of the road they were shot. My father told me of his admiration for a British chaplain, who was six foot six inches tall with bright red hair and helped those who struggled most on the march. I later read about this man's role in other stories of the march.[3]

My father walked about two hundred kilometers before being placed in the cattle trucks that were similar to those that took people to the death camps. He spent three days and nights without food, water, or toilet breaks with sixty people locked in one of the trucks. Some of these cattle trucks were then strafed by the Allies' planes.

Later, near the end of his life when he was dying from bowel cancer, he told me that he thought the cancer was as a result of the food that he had eaten on this march. They had dug from the frozen ground with their bare hands and eaten raw the turnips intended as cattle feed that grew along the side of the road.

---

3. Holliday, *RAAF POWs*.

As a kind of confession, my dad told me how he had decided on this march that he would never starve to death. He was saying that he had made a moral decision that he would steal food, and perhaps kill for food, before succumbing to starvation. He was telling me something of his will to live through that most difficult time and of a hierarchy of values that he had had to form.

As I read the stories of the great march, I wondered and then asked my father a rather naive, perhaps silly, question: "Were the Germans inhuman?" Without hesitation he said "No. There was a German officer whom we called 'Monkey-face.' The Allies strafed and burned his home and he shared his cake with me." This is to me a most extraordinary story. I used it in my dad's funeral to sum up the person he was. It is a Eucharistic story, which interpreted my father's life and shapes my identity and being. It reflects a deep recognition of and respect for the humanity in the other. I wonder how come I was gifted to have this man as my father. And, I have wondered for years why some people survive such difficult circumstances and always see the good in the other, while others become bitter and ill and die.

Subsequently my father "escaped" from prison camp. I use the quotation marks because he did. He said that it was near the end of the war, and that together with some others he walked out the front gate of the prison. He did not see this as a great act of bravery or heroism, for the war was virtually over and the Germans, he said, were really taking no notice. After having traveled some distance from the camp, German soldiers surrounded them. They thought they would be shot as escaped prisoners, but the soldiers were "looking for someone else" and let them go.

My dad made his way home to be reunited with his wife and son. Since my mother died when I was young I had no opportunity to find out her perception of these wartime events. I can only imagine. After such difficult times for both my mother and father, I imagine an anxious, relieved, joyous coming together. When I asked my father if I was conceived about the time of this reunion, he said, "Yes, ten minutes after!" And when I look at the dates of his arrival home and my birth it seems like his calculation was pretty close.

That is not the end of the reflection on this story for me. As you'll recall, this was a story about the shaping of my dad's prayer. Speculating on what might have happened in his mind during his time in prison and aware of how people in difficult situations bargain with God, I asked him:

"When you were in prison, did you come to an agreement with God that if you got home safely and had another child you would dedicate that child to God?" His response: "Yes, that's pretty accurate. That is probably what happened."

As I revisit these stories of my father, I realize that they help me to know something important about who I am in the present, they help me understand just what shaped my call to ministry, shaped my identity, and shaped how I live in marriage and as a parent. I know more confidently who I am as a pastor, as a spiritual leader, and as a priestly person when I tell these stories; they help me to live this difficult time of transition. They are stories that are about light out of darkness.

GOALS

My dad shaped me in other ways too. As a successful salesman, setting goals was an important part of how he was intentional in his living. Perhaps that early influence primed me for how the artist Vincent Van

Gogh lived his live with such intentionality. Vincent's letters to his brother Theo[4] are for me a "spiritual classic" to which I return often.[5]

Engraved on my heart are these words Vincent wrote to his brother: "I go on like an ignoramus but knowing this one thing: in a few years I must finish a certain body of work. I need not overhurry myself, there is no good in that—but I must work on in full calmness and serenity, as regularly and concentratedly as possible, as concisely and economically as possible. The world only concerns me in so far as I feel a certain debt and duty towards it because I have walked that earth for thirty years, and, out of gratitude, want to leave some souvenir in the shape of drawings or pictures—not made to please a certain cult in art, but to express a sincere human feeling."[6] And I marvel that in ten years he had produced an extraordinary body of work, and was dead.

It is likewise the call of Jesus that we live intentional lives, choosing to respond to the call to follow and to risk going where that call takes us. And so as minister, priestly person, and spiritual leader I try to model that intentionality for the people in my care.

One way I do this is by setting myself written goals. I tend to do this at key points, such as when I came home from sabbatical in 2002, when I lost my position in theological education, and when I began ministry in a new parish.

It may seem that my goals sound terribly rational, logical, and controlled while the lived journey is so often filled with emotion and uncertainty. Yet experience teaches me that the two work together. The intentionality of the articulated life goals becomes the armature on which lived experience finds its form, much as I paint with seeming abandon precisely because of the many hours I spend sketching and practicing, and much as a musician performs wonderfully before an audience only thanks to the many closeted hours of painstaking practice.

---

4. Roskill, *Letters*.

5. One of the great gifts "the church" has made to the world (I think,) is that it rejected Vincent's application to be a minister. He'd have been the fourth generation of Van Goghs to be a minister. Vincent had a passion to "bring light into darkness"; that is how he saw his call to ministry. He looked for the darkest place on earth, thought that would be in the bottom of the mines, and so set about ministering there. He only took up painting after the church had rejected him as a possible minister. I have read and like the suggestion that, through his paintings (particularly the later works) and in a far more significant way, Vincent managed to live out his ministry goal of "bringing light into darkness."

6. Roskill, *Letters*, 201–02.

Here, then, is an example of the kinds of lists I write periodically, this one made after my role in theological education came to an end. You will notice it is divided into areas: life goals, ministry goals, theological education goals, and goals as an artist.

Life Goals

- To live with integrity and responsibility the life and privilege given me as one who walks this earth.
- Like Vincent Van Gogh, to produce a body of work as an artist and as a minister that expresses my gratitude for the privilege of walking this earth.
- To live as one formed by the practices of the Christian faith.
- To be a marriage partner to Heather in such a way as I enable her to live the fullness of her being.
- To be a parent, father-in-law, and grandparent who is trusted and respected and who values and seeks to enrich the living of all family members.
- To live faithfully the ministry to which I am called.
- To be an artist of quality. To produce a body of work which because of its quality, has to be taken seriously (and from which I hope I can earn a partial income).
- To value and develop the gift that I have as a reflective writer, so being open to writing another book or books.
- To be fit and healthy . . . and so live a regular exercise program that nourishes my body, mind, and soul.

Ministry Goals

- To live faithfully the ministry to which I have been called.
- To practice my faith as ongoing life formation.
- To participate regularly in worship and the practices of faith.
- In the seven years of 'active' or paid ministry before possible retirement, to continue to make a contribution to the fields of

pastoral theology, art, and theology.

- To contribute to a renaissance of the arts and the expressions of the imagination in the church.
- To recognize that my ministry as a teacher in the field of pastoral theology at UTC is finished and to find another way to share those gifts.
- To be open to the way my life calls me forward, to use the gifts and integrity that I have within the church in whatever way the church may call me to use them.

Theological Education Goals

- To be a respected and trusted thinker in the fields of pastoral theology and theology and the arts. To do research that leads to exhibited paintings and published writings and that gives stature to my field.
- To be respected and trusted as a pastor and teacher.
- To facilitate adult learning.
- To be an innovative teacher, thinking seriously about (trans)formative learning.
- To maintain my network connections with people in the pastoral theology and theological education networks from around the country and overseas.
- To pursue an opportunity to be an artist-in-residence in an overseas seminary or church.

Goals as Artist

- To be an artist of quality. To produce a body of work which has to be taken seriously. Between the ages of sixty and seventy five, to produce a significant body of mature work. To earn a partial income from my painting that will support me in these years. To seek opportunities to be an artist-in-residence and to show work in significant spaces and galleries.

- To build and maintain a network of people in the arts who are willing to meet regularly to talk creatively, critically, and supportively about painting.
- To spend regular times in my studio.
- Always to push harder.
- To use better quality materials, as I am able.
- To draw daily, both the human figure and the landscape.
- And to PLAY whenever I am in the studio.

THE RETREAT

A number of months after I had lost my role as a seminary teacher I went away on an annual retreat with a precious group of friends.

Each year for thirty-plus years I have been away on retreat with the same group of colleagues. We eat well, drink good wine, yell a bit, tell jokes, worship, and each give an account of our life and ministry over the previous twelve months. Nothing is formally worked out; there is simply an expectation among the group that these things will happen and they do. In the best way, my friends were there for me helping me to find my way forward to a new ministry within the church.

At the time of this retreat I was confused, dispirited, lonely, and, hurting deeply.

The house in which we stay is in an isolated bush spot on the coast. You can stand inside with your backside to the log fire and watch the waves crashing on the rocks far below. A pod of humpback whales camped in the bay below us and frolicked there during our entire stay.

Having listened to each person give an account of his life and ministry in the previous year (that took a couple of days), we sat around the rustic log table beside the barbeque. Bathed in the sunshine and with the smoke of the burning eucalyptus, we shared communion. Robert read from the 104th Psalm that alludes to Leviathan whom God made for the sport (or play) of it. Then we listened to the reading for the week from Mathew 14 in which Jesus walks on water. Gregor reflected on the passage naming each of our lives and journeys.

I will confess I had come to this table in a dark mood. On the wooden picnic table there was Robert's Bible, a large bread roll that coincidentally had a cross in its surface from the way it had sat on the cooling rack, and a bottle of red wine from Brown Brothers, an old winery from the North East of Victoria. As Gregor talked about the water and about the risk taking needed to step out of the boat and to journey in faith, I could only think that the address on the side of the wine bottle would be Brown Brothers, Meadow Creek Road, Milawa. I knew because I had lived my primary school years on a farm at Meadow Creek and, except when in flood, that creek was a tiny trickle of water. It flowed through our property under the willow trees, a green oasis in the hot summer. It was the "body of water" that I knew; and it was by the waters of this creek that I first heard a "voice" call me to ministry.

Now in a time of pain and career uncertainty, I had been imagining a new space that I might inhabit in the future. In my imagination, that space came in the form of renovating and rebuilding the buildings on this childhood farm. There was to be a warm and light family room on the house and then a study studio beside the house.

As I became aware of these things, tears welled up inside me and then flowed down my face. I took my glasses off and tried to brush away the tears.

When we were done, when we had shared the bread and wine, we passed the peace to each other, me without words, for had I tried to speak the tears would have stopped me. I motioned to my friends that I wanted to speak, and tried to say that all the tears of the pain of the last year had finally welled up inside me and were now flowing. I alluded to the address on the wine bottle and the vocational importance of the waters of Meadow Creek for me. I shared my painful dilemma: whereas in the past that call has always been clear, now I could not see the way forward, and the pain of that was becoming more than I could bear.

Malcolm walked around behind me and warmly and tightly held my shoulders as I spoke.

All the while, the sun shone on us, and the whales surfaced and splashed and sprayed a couple of hundred meters away. With my words of sorrow and pain hanging in the air, we shared the remainder of the wine including a glass for our absent colleague, Nairn, who we knew to be dying. We drank and talked, then took Nairn's glass, and each in turn drank from it and told a story or made a blessing, such as Robert's, "May you be enabled to walk on the backs of the whales to the other side." I recalled how Nairn had not been part of this group for about ten years, but that when his mum died he came to be with us, and told us the story of her death. Though he maintained that he didn't understand why it was so important for him to be with us that year, to me it was obvious: we were his family, and he needed to tell us about his mum.

We drank together and blessed him: May his journey to death be quick and clean. May he be welcomed across the divide by his mum, and by Ferg—another member of this retreat group who had died seventeen years earlier, and whom we always fondly remembered and toasted during our annual gatherings.

It is a very special group of friends. I have met with them each year since I was the age my children are now. Yet for all the comfort and well being I felt in their company, I was distressed that I had no more clarity after the retreat about whether I wanted to be in pastoral ministry or even continue to be part of my denomination beyond attending weekly worship at my local church.

And so I wrote about that ambivalence:

"Hurting, uncertain, and yet somehow happy for the privilege that is my life."

CALL TO ST. IVES

That ambivalence persisted and was not quickly resolved.

The central church had suggested to me that I be in conversation with the St. Ives congregation with a view to becoming their minister. Yet I had imagined that I would spend the remainder of my working days as a seminary teacher and couldn't see my way through the fog to find a new direction. I couldn't make sense of what had happened to bring me to this point: for fifteen years before I had finally gone to teach at the seminary people had told me and asked me to prepare for being a seminary teacher. For nine years I had taught with only the most affirming response to what I was doing. I simply couldn't see another role for myself, not after all that. I didn't want to go back to pastoral ministry; not only did I not consider pastoral ministry the best use of my gifts for the church, I also didn't think that I had the energy to be a pastoral leader again.

There was another piece, too. I wanted to remain married to Heather, my beloved wife. As she had been the daughter of a minister herself and had spent her whole life moving from place to place because first her father and then her husband responded to a particular call, I couldn't see asking her to move—away from our own home, away from the garden she had lovingly created and tended, away from our children and (we hoped) future grandchildren, and away from the church where she felt that she belonged.

So perhaps you can understand why I was so uncertain about the Synod's proposal that I become minister of the congregation in the suburb of St. Ives. Having been burned, I didn't feel ready to commit myself to anything or anyone. I hoped (and people kept suggesting the possibility) that the denomination would see the error of their decision in letting me go, and reappoint me. It's a common hope after losing a job, and certainly I couldn't let go of that notion. Therefore I didn't want to close off that possibility by accepting the invitation of the church in St. Ives. And besides, I told myself, I had been invited to spend six weeks in Jamaica as part of a Faith and Culture exchange program and wasn't sure how life would look for me when I returned. So I asked the congregation to wait.

The congregation was also anxious. Their previous minister had left after just four months in the appointment; the manner of her leaving had left the congregation hurting.

No other opportunities opened up for me during that time away in Jamaica. I had decided that if the people of St. Ives church invited me to be their minister then I would accept their invitation and tell them as openly as possible of my anxiety.

And so I drove off into the darkness of the night, one lonely and uncertain minister, heading for a meeting with the selection committee of St. Ives parish. They had been very patient while I spent six weeks in Jamaica. I was still so uncertain. Yet earlier that day a friend from the United States had rung and said, "There will be something in this call that you can't yet see and it will use your gifts and be good for you." Another friend rang from interstate and reminded me that, "in each of your ministries something has been called out in you that you wouldn't have expected." I was grateful for those friendships and words of encouragement, and yet on the drive to the meeting I still anguished about committing myself to an unknown future. All I could do, I resolved, was to be honest about who I was, and then minister with integrity.

I arrived at the church and, rather symbolically, parked my car out in the street. I had resolved that if they were to ask me to be their minister I would say yes. But now, as I walked to the church door, I panicked: What if they had decided that they didn't want me?

Outside the room where I was to meet the selection committee I checked my clothes to be sure I was tidy. I discovered that I was wearing two belts on my trousers, one on top of the other. "That," I told the gathered church people, "reflects my anxiety and my uncertainty." I told them that if their invitation was still there then I would accept it. "Yet," I added, "I can offer no big plans. I can only promise to live honestly, openly, and deeply as your spiritual leader. I will love the people given to my care. I will lead the best worship that I am capable of. I will listen to the people of the congregation and the community. And I promise that I will not organize a mission statement!"

The selection committee recommended that I be called to the congregation. Because of their experience with the previous minister they were perhaps as anxious as I was.

A future in ministry was opening up for me, though at the time I wasn't terribly open to seeing its possibilities. Yet the night didn't seem as dark nor the journey as lonely as I drove home.

NEW GOALS AT ST. IVES

Accepting the appointment meant revisiting my life goals and becoming more specific about ministry goals in particular. So, when I began, what I had said to the selection committee were indeed my goals and therefore also my disciplines for ministry in St. Ives parish:

- To live openly deeply and honestly as a spiritual leader.
- To love the people given to my care.
- To lead the best quality worship that I can.
- To listen to both the people of the church and the wider community.
- To live into the ministry (slowly).
- To visit and to know the people and to let them know me.
- Not to make a mission statement. (Not to get trapped making ministry a management program.) I am not a CEO.

Some other related goals:

- To remain in and contribute to the field of pastoral theology: specifically, to participate actively and as often as possible in the Society for Pastoral Theology meeting in the United States.
- To be and to think as a theologian within the community.
- To do some tertiary teaching, as appropriate.
- To offer encouragement to lay and ordained leaders.
- To do some more thinking and writing on the pastoral imagination.
- To take some time to do my creative things, particularly painting and writing.

These goals and disciplines gave me a structure for the life ahead of me.

In a similar way to my being an artist, I have a long discipline as a pastoral person. It involves knowing my identity as a pastoral person, as a person of faith. It involves a capacity to attend to the experience of the other, to listen, to be present when I have no answers, to live with uncertainty, and ambiguity. In many ways it is similar to the discipline of artist. I learned about the tradition of faith in which I stand as I learned about art history and the tradition of painting. I learned certain skills for listening, for preaching, for leading worship, for chairing meetings and then I went into ministry, the "studio of life," where all I can do is "be." So being a pastoral person involves holding together all that I know and moving into a practice that involves being present when you have no answers, no things to say, when life demands more than you can give. It is in this space that, as a priestly person and a spiritual leader, I have to trust the images that emerge. In some miraculous way, the voice of God always breaks fresh into life.

The stories that follow are about being and doing in ministry. They tell of a continual revisiting and restorying of my identity, of a call or vocation that shifts, grows, changes. The disappointment and venom with which I began recording them has been tamed in the writing and rewriting. It has taken me years of deliberate rumination and simple getting on with the daily tasks in front of me to rediscover a hopeful and purposeful place in life.

The stories in varied ways reflect something of how I was to find light out of darkness. In retrospect, when I read these stories, I often have a sense that in each of these moments I was finding light that was giving my life new direction.

3

Being and Doing in Ministry: Doing

PRIESTLY PRESENCE[1]

SATURDAYS ARE TYPICALLY "MY" days. I read the paper, work in my studio, go for a thirty-kilometer bike ride, watch my football team, and get my mind ready for leading the people in worship on Sunday.

So when the phone rang at 9:30 a.m. to tell me that Ian, in hospital for tests, had taken a bad turn during the night and had ended up in intensive care, my whole day was thrown out in a way that it never had been while I was a seminary educator. I swallowed hard and reorganized my day so that I could drive across the city to see Ian.

As I drove I wondered about what I would do at the hospital and what would be expected of me. I've never been very comfortable in hospitals; I'd much rather talk with people in a coffee shop or classroom. I envisaged an uncertain amount of time standing beside a bed in intensive care. There would be machines, and tubes, and lights, and screens. I doubted that Ian would be able to talk with me. So I prepared myself. I thought I'd go in and say, "Ian, I've come to be with you for a while." I'd stay there for what seemed an appropriate time, offer a short prayer, and leave. It is my "priestly presence" that's needed, I reasoned to myself. But what precisely is priestly presence and what makes it so important?

Once in the ICU, I found Ian in his bed. He had on a full-face mask that was helping him with oxygen. He seemed pleased to see me and had much he wanted to tell me, only some of which I could comprehend, including a reference to the Good Friday service. Though I told him a few times that it was difficult for me to understand and I suggested that we just be still and be present with each other quietly for a time, he wanted

---

1. I have chosen to use the term "priestly presence" as a descriptor for one who symbolically mediates something of the presence of God. I come from a tradition where the language used to describe a spiritual leader is usually minister or pastor. Priestly presence seems to go further in indicating a particular symbolic function of and for the spiritual leader.

to be neither still nor quiet and went on telling me things that seemed important to him, yet which sadly I could not understand.

I stayed thirty minutes, said a brief prayer, and drove home, both marveling at the privilege of being called into someone's life at a time like this and wondering just what I had contributed. The one thing I had understood from Ian was that he wanted me to know something about the importance of the Good Friday service for him. He knew me as the person who helped him worship and who broke open the Word of God for him. Is this priestly presence?

Over the next two weeks I visited Ian in intensive care a couple more times, once after his son rang at 7 p.m. on Friday night relaying that Ian was asking for me, and could I come as the doctors expected him to die that night? Sitting comfortably at home, tired, and thinking of the security of my bed and a good book, I tried buying time: Would he be there tomorrow? No. So I drove across town again, knowing this time that I would be with a family saying goodbye to husband and father. Again I drove wondering what I would do, what I could say, and how my presence would make a difference. How would it be priestly?

It was a bit easier this time. Ian's wife, a son, and a daughter-in-law were beside the bed, waiting together for his imminent death. "We've been singing hymns with him," they told me. And after a reasonable passage of time and important conversation about their shared life, saying goodbye, and the appropriateness of their manner of being present to their husband and father in this most precious time, his wife asked me to pray.

On this occasion, priestly presence was about being with a family as they looked to find light in the darkness. My task was to be there with and for them and to somehow represent the light that comes from the darkness.

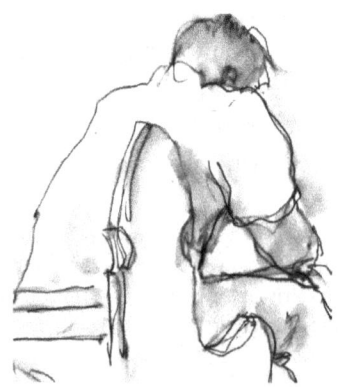

POLISHING THE SILVER

The question about priestly presence stays with me.

I retrieve from the drawer my antique portable communion set, passed on by an older minister to my wife's dad, and then to me. The leather upholstery on the box has long since disintegrated, the blue lining is quite faded, but the plate and goblets are silver and they still polish up well.

I'm not usually the one who polishes the silver, but this morning we are to take communion to Andy Anderson, a man in his nineties who has cancer and will likely die sometime in the next two weeks. He doesn't want any other visitors, just the minister and the pastoral care worker to share communion with him. I polish up the cups and plate thinking of the importance of this "last (earthly) meal" and Jesus' words from Mark 14 where Jesus, as he passed the cup to his friends said, "Truly I tell you, I will never again drink of the fruit of the vine until the day when I drink it new in the kingdom of God." It's a metaphor that hints at an existence I know only in faith.

Taking bread and wine to nourish an elderly man as he lives his dying, as he lives the fullness of his life, seems like an incredibly important task and privilege. For all of his life comes together in the sharing of this simple and symbolic meal. So this meal requires the best silver. As I polish, I wonder for a moment whether I will some day eat and drink my last earthly meal from this plate and these goblets.

I continue pondering as I polish. I don't know Andy well. He has only come to church a couple of times this year and only when there is communion. At this point in his life, he understandably hasn't wanted to meet new people.

So is *this* priestly presence—this piece of bread, this cup of wine, a short prayer, some physical touch, and a blessing?

As I write, I look out the window at a bird washing itself in the pool of water in my neighbor's gutter. I'm thinking: should I read scripture too? A psalm? Which one? Or should I just keep it short and simple and let the symbols do their work?

I wonder how many other people have eaten from this plate, drunk from these goblets. I wonder about their journeys.

I fill the silver flask with grape juice and buy a loaf of bread, from which I take one slice and place it on the silver plate within the well-worn case. The worn leather handle breaks as I close it.

Pam, the pastoral care worker, and I travel together to the nursing home to see Andy. Down long corridors hung with very ordinary "Sunday" paintings, past the staircase of the lovely old building that once was the home of Sir Roden Cutler, state governor and war hero, down one floor in an elevator, and finally along another dark corridor, where we are met by Jane. She is a neighbor of Andy's and has become his main caregiver. She has come to find us to tell us that he is a bit distressed because he hasn't been showered yet and is still in his dressing gown. On our way in, Pam had told me that Jane had said she wasn't sure about the God stuff for herself, but she is happy to be with us for communion.

We go into Andy's room. It is flooded with the late morning sun. Andy sits in his chair in the middle of the room, white legs extending beneath his red dressing gown. His face reflects the glow of the late autumn sunshine that fills the room. He seems so happy to have us there. Our peace is interrupted by Graham, a caregiver, who has come to give Andy a shower. Jane very clearly articulates that we are about to share communion, and asks him to return later. Someone calls on the phone, and again Jane creates space for us to share an intimate meal by asking the caller to try again later.

While we've been sitting there together, I've been asking Andy to tell me something of his life, to help him name his identity, because when you know who you are you can live the transitions. There's a photograph in the room of Andy and his wife, Phil, on their wedding day in London in 1940. He was an electrical engineer back then, responsible for keeping up the electrical supply to London during the bombing raids. "Some of those nights were difficult, 'bloody' even, if you will excuse the phrase," he tells me. His daughter, Joan, had migrated to Australia with her family and, after making four trips in five years to see them, he and Phil also migrated in 1989. It was so unusual for one so old to migrate, their move rated a story in the *Sydney Morning Herald*.

In the telling of his story, there are moments when Andy seems to stop mid-sentence, particularly when he's talking about emotionally difficult times, like the death of his daughter at the age of fifty and the death of his wife.

Jane fields another phone call, tells another party we're sharing communion. I open the battered little communion case and take out the silver goblets and plate. As I pour the wine I say to Jane, "I'm not sure of your practice, and don't want to embarrass you, but I invite you to share with us in the communion." "It doesn't embarrass me," she responds. "I went to a church school and did it then."

I offer a prayer of thanks for God's gift of life, for Andy's life, for life shared particularly with Phil and Joan, and for sustenance for his continuing journey. Then I quietly break the piece of bread and pass the plate to Andy, Jane, and Pam. I likewise pass around the wine in the silver goblets. I conclude with the Aaronic blessing, said particularly to and for Andy: "The Lord bless you and keep you, the Lord make his face to shine upon you and be gracious unto you, the Lord lift up his countenance upon you and give you peace, both now and for evermore."

We take our leave. Andy, ever the gentleman, wants to stand and walk us to the door. It takes three attempts for him to stand, but he does it.

My lasting memory will be of the light in the room and in Andy. And of Jane saying how special it was to participate in the communion, and how important she thought that it was for Andy. "Thank you for coming," she tells me. "It is a privilege," I respond.

FAYE

Faye was a much loved member of the congregation. The news that her cancer had returned in a virulent way was distressing for her, her husband Roger, her daughter Amelia, and for all the church and local people.

I had visited a few times and had been planning to visit her at home again on this afternoon, but she had been admitted to the palliative care ward in the morning.

I went to the hospital with some inner uncertainty and therefore was happy to drive around the block in the winter sunshine looking for a place to park. When I reached the hospital, I found it was the rest period, not visiting hours, and would have been happy to go and delay by sidetracking for a coffee the task of sitting with a woman who knows that she has come to hospital to die. There was to be no avoidance that day. "Third room on the right, second bed on the left," the receptionist told me helpfully.

Faye looked at me from under her hand-knitted beanie. She was clutching a much loved teddy bear. "Hello Doug. I'm feeling very weak." We made some small talk and I said, "Faye, don't feel you have to talk to me. I'm happy to sit here and be silent." A nurse came to insert an IV. She gave Faye some water, and at Faye's request, some ice too.

After fifteen or twenty minutes of quietly being together, Faye mentioned something about there being too many people. Taking the hint, I asked whether I could bless her and be on my way. "Please," she said reaching out her hand for me to hold while I invoked God's blessing on her. As I left she said, "I haven't known you for long, won't know you for long, but what I've met has been good, thank you." Her "goodbye" reminded me of my dad when he had his brain tumor. The wardsman brought Dad his clothes, and when he left the room he turned to Dad and said "Goodbye," to which my dad replied, "See you later. See you later. Thank goodness someone can say, 'Goodbye'!" Faye was clear in her "goodbye."

I left, wondering and marveling at her clarity and peace.

In the foyer I found Roger, Faye's daughter Amelia, and her daughter-in-law, Sharon, waiting patiently until the end of the rest period before entering her room. "How did you get in?" they asked. When I told them of my time with Faye I think they were glad that I had been able to be with her on my own.

Seeing Amelia with her red hair triggered a memory. "When I visited your mum at her home she said to me, 'I have been very angry at God, but not as angry as my daughter. If you see a woman coming towards you, red hair flowing, get out of her way. She's angrier with God than I am.' Well, that's appropriate," I said, "when your mother is dying." And we talked for some time about Faye, wife, mother, mother-in-law. Then Sharon volunteered, "She has been another mother for me." I mistook her to mean a second mother alongside of her mother, but she corrected me. "No, my parents were both killed in a car accident fifteen years ago and she has been my mother since then. She was the one I turned to when my children were born."

Those reflections were all a necessary part of saying goodbye, acknowledging a special person. "Sounds like what you have to say can be said in touch—a hug, a smile; words won't be able to say it all." And as I so often do in such situations, when family members are waiting for their loved one to die, not knowing when, not quite knowing what to do and how to be, I told them that people choose their time of dying. Sometimes they wait till everyone is there with them in the room, and sometimes they wait until you leave. Roger talked about Faye's mother, who had died three years earlier, and how she had sent her grandson out to get a coffee and when he came back he found her dead. This family understood.

Amelia asked if I thought her mother was at peace. "Yes," I said. I told them of blessing her and the subsequent conversation. "Anyone who can acknowledge me the way she did and say goodbye in the way that she did is at peace."

As I went to my car I thought: if Faye dies while I am on holiday, for the first time in my life, I'd be willing to come back to conduct her funeral and give my support to this family. What would that do to my marriage, I wondered, if I had to say to Heather, I am going back to the city for a couple of days to conduct Faye's funeral?

AT THE EDGES OF A FUNERAL

Faye did indeed die while I was on holiday. I had already talked with Heather about the importance of my returning to the city to conduct Faye's funeral. She understood that, having walked with Faye and her family, I wanted to be there.

So I drove the four and a quarter hours to Sydney to lead a service of thanksgiving for Faye's life, deliberately arriving at the church an hour and half early so that I could have a cup of tea and prepare for leading the service. The family had already swung into action, displaying numerous photographs of Faye, grandkids' drawings, and a couple of tables of symbols of Faye's life.

It seemed as if Pam, our pastoral care worker, had not experienced this sort of energy for a funeral before. But after all, as I explained to her, once the family used not only to wash and dress the body, but even to dig the hole in which their family member would be buried. We've pretty much lost all control of what happens to our dead family member nowadays; have put it all in "professionals'" hands. I have known ministers who have seen it as their sole right and responsibility to speak about the one who had died and not allowed the family's voice to be heard at the funeral service. I told the family that the service was for them to acknowledge the life of their wife, mother, and granny. They could do whatever would make it significant for them. I had suggested to them having a table of symbols and a photographic essay to remember Faye. So what they were doing was not only appropriate but also presumably cathartic or healing.

Before the service began I invited Roger to tell me about each of the symbols of Faye's life. That took a while, not only because Roger was nervous, but because he appropriately needed to tell the stories associated with those symbols in order to be able to name who he was on this most difficult day for him. At the beginning of the service I then stood at the tables and, based on what Roger had described to me, told the congregation how and why each item was important: "Faye's Brown Bear who knows all the secrets . . . the red jumper that Brown Bear wears that was knitted for granddaughter Caitlin when she was a baby . . . these small sheep reflect her role as a spinner and weaver . . . a brick with the name Spear on it from her grandparents' brickyard: all these items give a picture of the life of Faye who was cremated earlier in the week, and for whose life we now give thanks."

Funerals are demanding places and times. Often people are vulnerable to the memories and emotions of other times. There are so many people to be aware of, so many "life and death" conversations often grabbed in a few seconds and building on the conversations that have been had in other places.

It is my job as a minister to be alert to these conversations at the edge of a funeral. I see someone standing reflectively and quietly by themselves. I hear another mention more than once "the suicide of my brother when he was forty-five." I stand next to Richard for a few moments while waiting to begin the service, knowing that his wife had died from cancer, too, that he had been the "chief mourner" in a similar funeral. He looks pensive. "My guess is that days like this are particularly difficult for you." "Yes," he affirms and goes on to share his memories. "Barbara would have been the same age as Faye." And he talks of the help that having a recording of the funeral service had been for him in getting through the tough times over the years.

There's Brenda, whose husband had died suddenly nine months earlier. She's told me how she keeps herself busy because she is so lonely. I don't have to say much in order to recognize her journey, just "Hello, Brenda, thanks for letting me know about your test results." She turns from what she is doing and walks with me to the room where afternoon tea is being served and brings me a cup of tea—a gift acknowledging, "the unspoken knowing."

Over here are David and Muriel: David has been on dialysis two days a week for some time. Five days he can be out and about, then two days he spends at the hospital. I want to acknowledge that because it is his "cancer" and it can bring about his death at any time. As I stand with him and Muriel after the service I don't want to be trite, don't want to confine our conversation to talk about football. So I talk about Faye's anger at the cancer, "and I guess your anger at the kidney failure." "Yes," David acknowledges, and that leads to a conversation about the dialysis and the choice to sell their home and downsize to make it easier for Muriel in case David should die. Then we seemed to get sidetracked into talking about Muriel's brother who had died from cancer when he was forty-five, and the difficulty of that time, that his partner could not talk with him about his cancer and his dying, and Muriel's confession: "I still have difficulty forgiving her for that." The conversation named some other family concerns, and that leads to Muriel's unnecessary apology: "I don't know why I'm talking about this, sorry." "Because the funeral is about life and death, and what you are talking about is the stuff of life and death. It is appropriate that you talk about it; it's what happens when we open ourselves to what is going on at a funeral/thanksgiving service," I say, and David nods quietly.

Ivan, another member of the congregation and long time friend of Faye and Roger, stands at the back of the church looking lonely and forlorn, lost in his own thoughts. He reaches out his arms to me, making me think he's going to hug me. Instead he takes both my arms, holds them firmly, and thanks me for the service. His emotions are so close to the surface; holding them in check is difficult. I think we all live with the fear that if our emotions break out in the form of tears, we've somehow lost control and are less because of it. The reality is that in time, the tears pass, we breathe again, and life continues.

In the service I had wanted to acknowledge that Faye had died a "good death," even though both she and Roger had for a time been very angry with the cancer, and angry with God. She had moved beyond that, and could acknowledge and give thanks for relationships and say good-bye in appropriate ways.

As in every funeral, so too at this one there are the people that I do not know, that I have not met before. There is the woman who, with tears in her eyes, thanks me for what to her has been the most authentic, the most human, and the most appropriate (funeral) service. How in a word can I say something responsible, meaningful, and affirming to her by way of response? It is after all my hope that those who have come to the funeral will feel more affirmed in their humanness as they leave the service. That to me is the priestly task of blessing the people.

PREPARING A LAMENT SERMON

This Friday morning such blessing takes another form. The room is cold and my fingers struggle to work. I'd come aside to prepare a sermon for Sunday. I'd been thinking on it all week without getting very far. I'd tried to write in my journal to get focused and I kept getting distracted by the emerging painting on the opposite wall. So, in my good clothes I allowed myself to be diverted into putting more paint on the canvas.

My text for Sunday is Psalm 130: "Out of the depths I cry to you, O Lord." I'd read some commentary on the psalm. I'd read Kadi Bilman and Dan Migliore's book on lament[2] I'd recalled Herbert Anderson's lecture on lament at the Academy of the Rockies. And I'd been remembering the Society for Pastoral Theology meeting the previous week in Denver as part of which we visited Columbine and listened to people who were involved as parents, teachers, and health and community workers that tragic day in April 1999 when two boys shot and killed thirteen students and then turned the guns on themselves. I'd pondered Andy Lester's lunchtime address at the meeting, "Being Angry with God."

I return to the psalm and read it again. I don't ever seem to get much further than the first verse. "Out of the depths I cry to you, O Lord." And verse two: "Lord, hear my voice! Let your ears be attentive to the voice of my supplications!"

I think of the people who will be present at worship and of the events that might call out lament: for one, the tragic death of a husband and father, and for another the sudden death of a husband after so many years of marriage, and the subsequent loneliness; for others, the life-threatening illness of adult children. I think of Faye, who, at the too-young age of sixty-eight had just gone into a palliative care ward, and her words, "I have been very angry with God!" I think of her husband Roger. I think of Lawrence, whose thirty-three-year-old nephew died suddenly just a few days ago. I think of the futile murder of my wife's cousin days earlier. No explanations, just painful mysteries. I think of the less known things—the lost jobs, the work roles that demand difficult decisions and actions, of physical and mental illness, and so on.

How can I preach about lament and being angry with God without naming all the shitty things that these people know in their lives?

---

2. Bilman and Migliore, *Rachel's Cry*.

As I write this and shape these questions the process of preparing the sermon comes alive. I am distracted to look at the painting I have in progress with its heavy black lines that evoke lament for me. My paintings have been filled with the hard lament that I cannot easily put in words. The paintings seem, in part, to be a lament for the pain of my own journey, a lament for the contemporary world that I see headed to new forms of global slavery, and an open lament about finitude and mortality. I become distracted and slowly read the words of the psalm yet again, then pick up Walter Brueggemann's commentary[3] and read what he thought about the psalm. I find a board and a large sheet of paper, and began to scribble notes.

I want to be aware of the lived experience of the people to whom I will be speaking, and at the same time I want to respect their experience of encountering the "shitty" stuff of life, and their "crying from the depths."

Behind me the painting is coming to life. I look at the yellow I had put in it and recognize: this painting is about Psalm 130. In the darkness of the cry from the depths is always the hope that if we wait for the Lord, the Lord will hear and respond, and that the things that are happening at the moment are not as they will be, but life will be transformed.

3. Brueggemann, *Message of the Psalm*.

About 11 a.m. I decide to go out into the cold of the day for a bike ride of a couple of hours—a time to think over the material for the sermon, to rehearse the preaching of it as I ride. An image comes to mind that will carry the sermon. Not an easy image, but perhaps enough humor to help people without it all becoming too serious.

In an earlier time I had lived in the church manse right next door to the church. The house was on a corner block and most people who knew us came to the back door—it was easier for them. Whenever the front door bell rang it was usually someone who wanted the minister to give them a relief handout. This particular evening I was preparing dinner for friends. They were about to arrive, and since they hadn't been to our home often I figured they would probably come to the front door. The doorbell rang at about the time I expected them. So I wiped my hands and went to the door to greet them. Instead of the friends I was expecting, a middle-aged man in dirty, disheveled clothes, and with a speech impediment stood there saying, "I yheet m'pants. I yheet m'pants!" It took me a few times before I understood. He was saying "I (have) shit my pants!" His was a genuine cry of lament from the depths, from the shitty place of life. How could I respond? He was asking for help; he wanted to come into my home, to use the bathroom, use the toilet, get cleaned up, and get a clean pair of trousers. Inside I was saying something like, "Oh my God, what am I going to do? This guy wants help, I'm in the middle of cooking a meal for people who will arrive any moment, and this guy wants me to do what only a mother would be willing to do. And he is waiting in hope that I will help him."

This story would provide an opportunity to talk about the address to God from the depths, from the really shitty places of life. It would allow me to talk about how only a mother—like God—could be so forgiving as to hear the cry of this man and act. And the man was waiting, hoping I'd be willing to help him. That likewise is the trust of the psalmist whose soul waits and hopes.

Twenty-four hours passed. Faye died. The story I had been so keen to use in my sermon twenty-four hours earlier now seemed inappropriate, out of place. I couldn't remember why I had been so keen to use it and how it was supposed to help. Preaching is about helping the people glimpse God, not showing them that I can tell a funny story. I became uncertain how best way to present the material.

When Sunday morning arrived I became even more uncertain as to how to speak the words in a way that would break into the faith lives of the people in relevant ways.

I had rehearsed the sermon so many times. Finally I resolved that I would go to church, stand in front of the people, and speak it. How would I bring it to a conclusion? I would link the cry from the dark and shitty places of life with the welcome at the Lord's Table where we are all accepted and nourished for our daily living.

When Sunday morning came I stood up and spoke, still not certain as to whether I should use the story. Halfway through the sermon I looked at the people and could hear myself stop speaking for twenty seconds while I decided, yes, the story would be appropriate. It was helpful in naming the cry that comes from the shitty places in life. When people came forward for communion they had a glint in their eyes and smiles on their faces and I seriously wondered if there was some joke that they all knew about that had somehow passed me by. I think they were glad that I had spoken honestly and used a word that we don't usually use in polite conversation, a word that spoke into the shitty places of their lives.

A NEW PAINTING

It is hard to know when I begin or finish a painting. Last week, while pulling out work for my forthcoming show I found a bundle of half a dozen paintings that delighted me. That is, they delighted me until I put them up in front of the friend I'd asked to help me select appropriate work for an exhibition. He was pretty clear that they didn't work: "The black and white parts don't breathe, don't work together, they don't go anywhere," he had said. "The paintings are too young. They need more work."

I played with one or two, taking them an extra step. But something remained disquieted within me. I wanted to reach out to create new marks. My mentor in the United States, Tom George, had written of some of my recent paintings: "I enjoyed seeing the small acrylic paintings. Simpler, more powerful and more direct than previous efforts—I respond to clarity and power, but a strength under both emotional and technical control—I don't mean a too consciously laid on scheme, but an effort both free and exact in intensity. A very hard order but one we find in every great master." That had excited and encouraged me, given me confidence to want to paint new work. Tom and I have related for many years and when he doesn't like my work he is silent, other times he offers hints for finding my way forward, still other times his response excites me and I want to paint.

I wanted to take into me the things Tom had said, and to make new paintings. The small works he had commented on were works I had made while on holiday when I didn't have other things to attend to. For now, I had a limited number of canvases and paints and had to work with what I had at hand. I wasn't trying too hard to make things happen, and I knew that I had the whole week to push and play. In the studio at home, with other claims on my time, I often push too hard; I want it all to happen too quickly.

The week and weekend had been busy. I had led a retreat for a congregation on Saturday and preached on Sunday. Monday I was looking after my two-year-old granddaughter. We had hurried back from the park because of an impending storm. When we got home she had wanted to sleep, so I had some time to paint.

I took two of the paintings on plywood (each 100 cm x 100 cm) that a week ago I had felt were good, joined them together as a diptych, and painted over them. Suddenly I was seeing the drawn line come to life in my paintings in ways that hadn't been evident before. As I looked at the work, I thought I had made "the Zen marks" that an artist friend had talked about in an earlier conversation. But instead of being patient and letting the marks rest, I raced on—and destroyed those beautiful marks. Then as I worked on I thought that I could see the balance between the absolutely free and the emotional and technical control that Tom George had talked about.

I couldn't stop painting this work. I painted after dinner when I was tired and I made a mess. When I looked at it next morning it was a monotone. So with a brush loaded with black paint I put marks all over the painting, wondering what would happen if only I could slow down.

A little time reflecting on other things in my journal and I looked up and could see why I should have slowed down; I really wanted just three or four lines in the painting and I had made hundreds of little black marks that made the painting far too busy.

I thought of Tom George's Chinese brush drawings, and I got out some images of his work and looked. It was so obvious that the Zen mark had become a discipline that informed all his subsequent work, an extraordinary discipline shaping the practice of a great artist.

I wanted to take my conversation with Tom further. How, I wondered, does Tom come to the moment of making a mark? I put one of his Chinese calligraphy works on the wall where I could be influenced by the stillness and deliberation of the hand that held the brush. He was so carefully intentional, so controlled and yet so free.

I worked on the painting again. A subtle balance of line and color. It seemed to have a dead spot in the top right hand corner. It was sort of "clunky."

I hung the work on the lounge room wall and looked hard waiting for the painting to tell me how to take it forward the next step.

I got a carefully and empathically worded e-mail from my editor telling me that the latest publisher had decided to pass on this book. I worked on my Father's Day sermon and I took the painting from the lounge room wall and continued to paint.

Saturday came and I had a whole day I could spend however I wanted. Most of the day I would spend in the studio, with a couple of hours out on my bike, rehearsing Sunday's sermon.

The painting had come to be very "landscapey." As I looked I could recall where I sat while on holiday and the half dozen watercolor paintings that I had done of the same scene. The temptation was to become more literal. Yet that would amount not to listening for how the paint would call me forward, but rather how I remembered the landscape, and thinking on the logic of how a landscape should be—such as that the water should reflect the colors and lines above it. So then I was painting what I thought the painting should look like rather than what it was. In a flash I had chosen to make it a landscape painting reflecting the literal of what "should" be there. This was not my normal way of painting, though it seemed at the time that that was what the painting was calling out in me.

I sat down to think:
What if

- I changed the color?
- I broke open the lines from the literal to the abstract?
- I rubbed paint off?
- I left it alone for a few weeks?
- I turned it upside down?
- I painted over it and began again?
- I made myself a coffee and came back and played on the surface?
- I took some white paint that was watery and ran it over the whole surface? Then rubbed it back with a cloth to see what emerges and take my hint from there?

I determined that the work had become too literal, so I stood up, took a brush and washed white paint over the whole painting, then made black lines following some of the old lines and some of the gestures made with white paint. I changed the music I was listening to from the jazz clarinet of Artie Shaw to the Abbey music my friend Terry gave me after his recent trip to Europe.

I wondered if the painting required more black lines. I drank my coffee, and thought. It was now such a different painting, yet another metamorphosis. I had liked it enough in its previous form to hang it on the lounge room wall for a few days, but now it did not quite work. The harder I looked, the less it satisfied. I had brought it to the studio intending to do one or two things but those one or two soon became three or four and I had gone too far. I liked the three simple lines now that I had made with a broad wiry brush.

I had painted over some lines, making them appear as shadows. It no longer mattered, for all that I had had was gone. The task was to listen. I picked up the broad wiry brush, dipped it in black paint and dragged it through some of the lines.

I tried to break myself free. I knew that if I had any sense I would put my brushes down and go for a long bike ride and come back when the paint had settled and begun to dry. I couldn't let go. I reached out to put more marks on the work. Every new mark changes the whole.

I was forcing myself out of the studio. I had my coffee cup in hand to take to the kitchen sink and I reached out and took up the wiry brush yet again and made some more lines in the painting. Were they help or hindrance? Not certain.

I forced myself to walk away. The bells in the Abbey music were reaching into my conscious self.

I went for the bicycle ride, came home, had lunch, and read the paper. I worked over the painting yet again and felt that it was beginning to beat me. I chose to have one last attack (the military language surely wasn't accidental!) I chose to get a lot of white paint, a big brush, and to go at it as hard as I could all over again. Then, I thought, I will go and watch the football game and sleep.

That is what I did and the gestures that I made in three, perhaps five minutes, all built on what had been there before. I took the painting and laid it flat on the floor so that the wet paint didn't run too far. I went to watch the football and I fell asleep.

Later I put the work on the wall and sat with gentle jazz on the radio, a whisky in hand, and looked at it. And I liked it. It worked. All the previous layers were somehow there and the spontaneity or "Zen" of the last few minutes had become the strength of the work. Very subtle blues, and oranges, and lots of greys. Vincent Van Gogh had said "There are but three fundamental colors—red, yellow, and blue; 'composites' are orange, green, and purple. By adding black and some white one gets the endless varieties of greys."[4]

The biggest questions of all remained: Will it still please me in the morning? Will I have the confidence to leave it as it is?

I called the painting Agonis and I still liked it in the morning.

THE WEDDING INTERVIEW[5]: WHAT IS MY ROLE?

This time I did wait. I had to. I waited at home a half an hour after the due time for a couple to arrive for a pre-marriage interview, a wait that wasn't

---

4. Roskill, *Letters*, 158.

5. For closer detail on the wedding interview process described here see Purnell, *Conversation as Ministry*, 117–27.

a chore because I was watching my football team on the television, and they were winning.

The couple had been referred to me from outside the church; they wanted a minister to conduct their wedding in a reception center. I resolved that this would give me some contact with people outside of the church and I needed to do that.

Meeting people for the first time is always difficult, especially when I am to reach into the intimate space of their lives: getting married. So I asked them to tell me how they met. Maureen was the bride and she was full of energy, and told me how they had met on an Internet dating program. "It was a good program because it gave you lots of information about the other person; it enabled you to have some telephone conversations before you met." She told me how she had been up front and had said what she was interested in, such as settling down to have a family, and that she was looking for a partner who was interested in the same thing.

Initially, Nic, the groom, was a bit reticent, and let her do the speaking. I asked him where they first met and what his memories of that meeting were. Eventually, we got into some conversation, though it wasn't easy.

I have official forms that I have to fill in and they ask for lots of details about the people: Where and when they were born, who their mum and dad are, whether they are living or not. So, using the forms as a prompt, I began asking the questions of him because that's how the form does it. I learned that Nic's parents had separated when he was sixteen. All of the other siblings had gone with his mum, and he had gone with his dad. His dad had died ten years ago and had bequeathed Nic his home. Nic still lived there. I asked Nic the date of his dad's death; it was one week before my dad died and so I had a way to connect with him.

When I asked Nic about his dad's death, he told me that his dad had died of lung cancer. Then, he rather passionately told the story. His dad had been at home, but on this day he had had to go to the hospital. He was kept in the waiting ward, then eventually was attended to, placed on a trolley—and left in a hallway. They told Nic that they were going to give his dad morphine to relieve the pain. Nic's view in retrospect is that they used the morphine to kill his dad. I tried to suggest that it was normal practice to give people morphine to relieve the pain and that doctors would be very vulnerable if they overprescribed the morphine to the point where it killed someone. Since that time, Nic told me, he had seen a lot of television shows that suggested the opposite is true. And he now understood. "On that day, I was so angry, I could have killed someone." Later that night, apparently, without having being admitted to the hospital, Nic's dad died in the hospital. His father's treatment was, from Nic's telling of the story, inadequate and distressing for the family. I thought it important to get Nic to tell as much of the story as he could. To tell the story is to name his identity and that helps with the grief, and enables him to enter the marriage.

This was a first interview and I moved on to tell Maureen and Nic about the wedding service itself, for example, the options for the bride in entering the space where the wedding will take place. I suggested a number of possibilities including the possibility that they might walk in together, or that Maureen walk in with her mum and dad together. I told them that while the TV shows still included it, there is no option in our service for giving away of the bride. I told them that that related to a previous time when women were the possession of men and usually passed on with a bride price. It would be important for me in the service to name their parents and to give them the opportunity in the service to give a blessing on the marriage.

Nic told me that he had said to his mother who had long ago remarried and had had two children in the second marriage that she would be known at the wedding by his father's name, and she had agreed with that. Then he said that his (deceased) father would be present at the wedding and there would be a place set at the bridal table for him. I became quite concerned when I heard these things: they seemed inappropriate, and seemed to indicate that he had not grieved appropriately for his dad. I struggled for the words and I said that I thought that it was inappropriate to provide a place at the bridal table for his dad. I told Nic that I thought it appropriate that his dad be mentioned, that perhaps they could light a candle at the beginning of the reception and acknowledge that though his dad had died and all are sad he isn't here to share this day, we remember him, and he is present in spirit. I suggested that he could mention his dad in his speech, and he told me that he intended to do that. I struggled a bit when Nic said, "Tell me why it's not appropriate to have a space set for him at a chair at the bridal table?" He suggested an alternative, that he have a photograph of his dad on the bridal table. Again, something within me reacted. I wondered inside about what was culturally appropriate, I wondered if I was being unreasonably conservative. I suggested to Nic that it seemed to me that what he was doing was not healthy. "What do you mean, 'not healthy?' Be straight with me." I was trying as hard as I could to be straight and clear but evidently I wasn't getting through. I suggested to Nic that this was not a healthy way to begin a marriage and that although it was his wedding and he would be able to do what he wanted to do, I saw my role as asking important (and difficult) questions when I thought it appropriate to do so. "I hope that in the car on the way home you will talk some more about these things. You can say you didn't like what that minister said. My role is to know what makes marriage work and what inhibits marriage and so I am here to ask significant questions to help you in the best way that you can for your marriage." Again, Nic asked me to "be straight." I struggled around inside to think how could I explain all that I know about grief and marriage in the simplest way possible.

I sought to be self-revealing. "My mum," I said, "died when I was seven years old. So when I married I was in many ways looking for a mother more than a wife. The crunch came when we had small children and my wife said to me, "I can't be mother to you and to your children, too. Something will have to change." It wasn't his mother who had died, and he asked me whether I thought he was looking for a father in his marriage? Perhaps he was, but it wouldn't have made sense to say so.

I was reaching hard to find something appropriate to say. So I asked "Who will be present in your marriage bed?" he answered "Why? Me and Maureen, of course." Perhaps It would have been better had I asked "How *many* people will be present in your marriage bed?" In some ways, that is what I meant. Again, I sought to explain my concern that setting a place at the bridal table for his dad or placing a photograph on the bridal table of his dad who had died ten years before suggested that maybe his dad would be present with him in the marriage bed too. Again he asked me to "be straight with him." I found it difficult to be clearer than I was being. I arranged a second interview when I would talk with them both about their experience in their family of origin and how that would likely shape their marriage. In my head I gave up on this for the day, and suggested that we might find ways to deal with it when we meet the next time.

Here is the dilemma: If Nic had come to me, saying "I'm struggling with grief over my father's death, will you help me to work it through?" I could have responded in quite different ways. But instead Nic and

Maureen had come asking me to conduct their marriage. They were not consciously interested in talking about unresolved grief. Yet I know that unresolved grief will shape their marriage in ways that are not healthy and that could lead to a marriage breakdown. During the conversation I had asked Nic, "How did you choose to be married?" His choice was very clear: "Because I want to have children and I want children to be brought up properly in a family. I don't want a broken family like my parents had. My brother got married and the marriage broke up. Then he had a relationship with someone and had three children but he was not married. Then that relationship broke up. I'm getting married because I don't want my relationship to break up and I want children to be brought up in the proper way."

I asked what shaped his values about marriage and family. Nic didn't understand my question and again asked me to be straight with him. So I asked, what shaped your understanding of marriage and of doing the right thing before God? (This was to use his language.) These were difficult questions for him.

During this conversation it transpired that they had had quite an argument in the car on the way to the interview. Maureen had been reading the map and had taken them on a very circuitous route that meant they had got lost and were half an hour late. In retrospect, I thought that might have been an expression of her anxiety about being married. It was very clear that both of them had reached a stage in life where they wanted to be married, were delighted that they had found a partner who wanted to share marriage, and family, with them, and were committed to doing it in the best way possible. Both had acknowledged that they had had a number of (significant) relationships before.

Who am I and what is my role as a minister when I conduct a wedding? Am I simply a liturgist who says the words of the ritual in the simplest way possible? Am I simply a clerk for the government, who fills in and signs the forms appropriately? Am I a pastor, priest, educator, healer whose responsibility is to work to help people live the difficult transitions of their life in the best ways possible? What happens when my expectation of my role in the wedding is different from the expectations held by the people who come to be married?

What is my role?

THE HELICOPTER WEDDING

The wedding that followed this and other conversations pushed me, too.

I don't get many weddings at my church and am delighted to be present in the significant events of people's lives. I wanted to be with people who are not part of the church to get some feel for the lives of people "out there." And I see my role as being different from a civil celebrant in that I bring the blessing of God to the people.

Each time Nic and Maureen came to see me they were twenty to thirty minutes late. I told them that my time was valuable and I'd appreciate if they could be at the wedding on time. If they intended to be late, they should let me know and I would come late, too; it would be easier for me. No, said Nic, we are getting ready for the wedding at the place, then Maureen will drive a few minutes away where she will board a helicopter that will bring her to the wedding. I thought they were joking, but I was wrong.

I had led morning worship and come home for a quick lunch before driving to the reception center. While it was only fifty kilometers (thirty miles) away, it took nearly an hour and a half to get there. I was there in plenty of time for the 3 p.m. wedding and sat in my car listening to the radio play-by-play of my football team and I watched the guests arriving in their low-cut, vibrantly colored dresses, push-up bras, and stiletto heels. Then at twenty minutes to 3:00, I went in to the reception centre, put on my alb and stole, and began the wait. The director of the center came to apologize, telling me that the bride would be half an hour late. I swallowed hard. I became angry, and I knew that the service would be rushed and tense.

There was the deep throbbing sound of a couple of Harley Davidson motorbikes as the groomsmen arrived. The groom arrived in a big Mac truck, a prime mover, highly polished, bright red, a wedding ribbon stretched across the hood. There was a similar truck behind it for the bridesmaids.

Why was I there? What was I doing? I was in other people's spaces, bringing a blessing for their wedding. But was that blessing anything more than superstition to them? I introduced myself to the father of the bride. He had two small dogs on leashes that were to be dressed and become part of the bridal procession. I told him that it was important for me to acknowledge both him and his wife, and said that I would ask them during the service for their blessing on the marriage. Marriage is at least a two-generational event I told him, as important for you as for your daughter.

I went back to the balcony where the wedding would be held and talked with Samantha, who had brought a cage full of doves to release after the couple had been married. We were both a bit frustrated with the long wait. After half an hour had elapsed and there was still no sign of the bride, Mark, the manager, came to tell me that they had just heard that it would be another half hour. His chef was furious, he said. How do you slow down the preparation of a meal for this many people? What about the other staff with other commitments?

At 4 p.m. came the welcome sound and then sight of a red helicopter. It landed very close by. We waited ages for the rotor blades to stop turning. The bride got out. It took another ten minutes to travel the thirty meters to the place of the wedding with nine flower girls, three bridesmaids, two dogs, and a three-year-old page boy carrying the rings.

I stood talking with the best man while waiting for the bride to make the walk. He wanted to know if I had had one of my mates conduct my marriage. He was called to task by his mates for talking to the priest, as though this were a taboo conversation. "Why?" he said, "I've never had a chance to talk to a priest before. I want to find out." I asked the groomsmen to point out to me the mother of the bride. One made childish jokes about the size of one of the bridesmaids. Silly nonsense for men who were close to forty.

The wedding was now seventy minutes later than expected. I had family coming to my home to share a Father's Day celebration. What could I cut from the service? Not much. It was important for me to do the service appropriately and with dignity. I chose to drop the homily. I thought that the people who had been standing around for all this time would be too frustrated to hear anything and that my words would be lost on the wind. The helicopter had to leave before the service could begin. Noise and fumes.

Finally the music began, page boy, and flower-girls, bridesmaids, dogs, and the bride made their entrance and stood in rows in the tight space on the balcony. The service began. I introduced myself and attempted to interpret parts of the service as we went through it. The "purpose of marriage" statement sounds so special in church, but here seemed to have no relevance. I asked the families for their blessings, which were warm and generous. I invited the gathered group to express their support of the couple by answering my question to them with "we will." They were loud and enthusiastic in their support. Then Nic and Maureen held hands, and at my leading said their vows clearly and confidently. I declared them married. I told the gathering that the important thing that I do in this service is to bring the blessing of God. I will use simple words, I said, a twenty-five-hundred-year-old prayer. What all of us together are saying in this prayer is that we want the very best of all that God is and can be, for the couple in their marriage. I turned to the couple, held my outstretched hand over them and said the Aaronic blessing. It did seem an important moment.

Nic had been anxious when we last spoke that I should announce when he could kiss the bride, and I told him that this was the moment and the people could applaud. He didn't want to stop kissing her. Finally I told the gathered people that we would pray for the newly married couple and the life they will share. This was much harder. The couple talked all the way through the prayer. I sensed over my shoulder from the noises that the couple was continuing the kiss. The prayer seemed to me empty words. No one was listening or participating. The moment was gone. The prayer concluded with the Lord's Prayer that I invited others to share. I could hear no other voices. I pronounced the benediction and invited Samantha to release her doves. It was a nice moment. Bride and groom held the doves, were photographed kissing as they did so, and on the count of three released them. Then the flower girls were invited to open a big crate and to release a further dozen or so birds.

My patience was gone. I got the forms signed as quickly as I could, withdrew, and removed my stole and alb. One of the staff offered me a glass of wine. I said no thanks, I would have one when I get home. The groom apologized a couple of times for the delay. Then I was gone, heading for home, family, and a quiet drink.

So had this wedding been a waste of my time? Was I being used as just part of an economic transaction? It intrigues me that there are no Bible stories of Jesus inviting people into his home, except perhaps John 14, which seems to be an invitation to a "heavenly home." The stories are all of Jesus accepting the invitation to go into the home of the other. The stories that are told seem to reflect Jesus impressing the people present by his ability to find, see, and use the ministry moment.

My first reaction was: I am never going to put myself in this situation again. My time is more valuable than this. How could I charge a penalty for such a late arrival? It is only with the passage of time that I have begun to think more about entering the space of the other, bringing the blessing of God, being available for someone to have a conversation with a "priest." It was important to do, and, I would do it again if asked.

NOT SUPPOSED TO KNOW

It was raining heavily when I got in my car to visit Jack and Glenda. Some in the congregation had let me know that they were having a hard time with one of their adult children, "but it is confidential, you aren't supposed to know."

Over the years one of the hardest things for me as minister and spiritual leader has been when I am "not supposed to know." This day was like that. Earlier in my ministry I'd have been paralyzed by such a condition put on shared knowledge. I wouldn't have visited. I wouldn't have offered care. "How can I," I'd have said, "when I'm not supposed to know?" I have learned that it is important that I act, even if I'm not supposed to know. Yet there is always anxiety for me in these visits. How am I going to raise the matter that I'm not supposed to know about?

Glenda offered me a cup of tea, and went to get it. Jack talked about the work of one of his kids. The cat wandered into the room to sit by the radiator, and was gently removed and eventually put outside in the rain. I got a cup of weak black tea. We talked the very general stuff that was important for its preparatory function in the conversation, but of no consequence. I thought maybe they'd have guessed about my coming, because I had visited them just a few weeks before. If they did, they certainly didn't let on. Eventually I thought, "This is up to me; if I don't raise the matter they never will."

So I dived in: "I've come because your friends have told me that you have been having a tough time in your family lately. I have no idea what it is, but they suggested it might help if I visited." There was a stunned silence while they looked at each other. At first a bit of denial, then slowly, "Oh that must be about Jason. He's been a bit depressed lately." Glenda said that in praying about it, she had remembered that she had become depressed when she had cancer and that the local general practitioner had helped her by listening and prescribing appropriate drugs. She had suggested to Jason that he might see the doctor and with his agreement had made an appointment, and that seemed to have made a big difference. His behavior has changed and he is relating much better now.

My role was to get them to talk, for me to listen, and eventually to hold their concerns before God. In so doing I would be saying, "You are not alone in this, and together we stand with these difficult life issues before God."

In the beginning I guessed they were not telling me all there was to tell. Slowly and gently they let me know about the journey with Jason; the pain of his broken relationship and some of his difficult behavior. Jack said quietly, "It has been a difficult time for us." I listened. Occasionally we drifted away from talking about Jason and when it was appropriate, I refocused the conversation by summarizing the things they had said and asking "gentle" questions.

I had a time limit because I'd arranged to visit someone else that day. When I thought that we had named the "difficult time" appropriately (though probably not completely), I offered to pray, an offer they warmly accepted. I held them and Jason before God, asking for wholeness, healing, and purpose in Jason's life, asking a blessing on his new relationship, and asking God to hold and sustain Jack and Glenda through this time. "Give them the grace and energy to be supportive parents." When I finished praying I looked up and Jack was using both hands to wipe the tears from his face.

When I got up to go, Jack found ways to touch me warmly, shaking my hand, putting his hand on my shoulder, and telling me they were grateful because this had been of concern to them.

I didn't want them to be alone in this time. It is why we are a community; it is what I do as a priestly person.

It was still raining when I left.

LISTENING TO LIVES SPEAKING

The coordinator of the multiple sclerosis support group that meets monthly in our church had invited me to come to meet the people. I went in, was introduced to each person in turn, then sat down at a table and tried to engage the group in conversation. The woman to my right was in a wheelchair and was keen to tell me about her life. She had been in Christian ministry before being confined to the chair. She had, she told me, managed to conduct a couple of weddings from the chair; they were for close members of her family. I wanted to know something about each of the people at the table, so I looked across the table and invited Dave to tell me about his life. "What did you do to earn money before you retired?" I asked, expecting an answer of one or two sentences. But the answer never stopped. I heard how after he finished school he was encouraged to go to teacher's college, got a position in the country, then had a teaching exchange with someone in the UK, whom he still knows, came back and completed a degree. And then somehow I was learning about his son going on a student exchange and on and on without a break. He needed to speak. Yet I was looking for a pause so that I could also ask the other people about their lives, so after about fifteen minutes I broke in and said, "I'd like to ask Graeme about his life, too."

Some time later I learned that the first symptoms for Dave of his MS was that he had difficulty with his vision. In short order he had retired from his position in tertiary education. Books had been his life and he could no longer read. He lost his mobility, too, and could no longer drive a car. One day he went out on public transport and he couldn't recognize where he was, and since then, for his own safety, he rarely ventures out on his own. Now he manages a short walk with his walking frame to the nearby coffee shop where he and his desire for a cappuccino are known. With the loss of sight, inability to read, and restriction in mobility, he stopped being in social networks that stimulated his mind. No wonder that when someone asked about his life he was ready to talk.

Years ago the church in which I ministered had a daily lunch for senior citizens, and I would sit each day and talk with people about their lives. These people mostly lived alone in nearby apartments and needed the social contact. Over a number of years I had some wonderfully rich conversation with them.

Here, eating curried egg sandwiches with folks suffering from MS, I was a bit taken aback by their need to have airspace. I wanted to be present to them—that is what I think ministry is about. Only "being present" was tougher than I had anticipated. Probably I had gotten out of practice. I remembered some tough conversations with some deeply hurting people in the past. Back then, I had built a relationship with those people and over time had visited most of them in their apartments, been for weekends away with them, sat and talked with them, led them in worship, visited them in hospital, and had spoken at the funerals of their friends. I had become trusted and was given access to the deep parts of their lives.

This day was different. This day I was meeting people for the first time. I was inviting people to tell me something about them and Dave was certainly going to tell me as much as he could in the time available. To be present to people while they talk about their lives is to value their souls. So maybe the only relevant question is how I can affirm the importance of Dave's experience as a person suffering from MS and value and acknowledge all that he has done in his life rather than become impatient myself and want to move on to the next person and her story?

In this morning's newspaper was an interesting article comparing a society that was driven by economic rationalism with a society that might be driven by the valuing of relationships that people have with others and their connectedness to geographic space. Jesus, I thought, didn't talk too much about the profits returnable to the shareholders. Ministry, for him, was about relationships and about being present to and engaging the lived experience of the other.

4

Privilege

MINISTRY HAS EXTRAORDINARY PRIVILEGES. Last night Bev White rang and asked if I would visit her husband in hospital. We hadn't met. Bev lives next door to one of my parishioners. They are good friends, and when Bev's husband John was diagnosed with a terminal illness I was recommended as a "good conversation partner." Bev and John had wanted to come to church to meet me, but the illness had overtaken their intentions.

As I drove to the hospital I wondered: What can I do or say when meeting people in circumstances like this, when I don't know them, when they are not part of my church community? Because they had rung me, I knew that they wanted something from me, even if I was not sure what it was. This was to be a reading, writing, thinking day so my time was free and flexible. Probably I'd spend fifteen minutes—half an hour tops—with them.

Both John and Bev were expecting me. But when I walked in John was having the IV drip moved from one arm to the other. The nurse was new and making rough weather of the task. The pain must have been awful for John was in tears; yet, knowing she was new at the role, at the same time he was encouraging her.

I was offered a chair and sat while the nurses worked on his arm, while a doctor came and went, and while Bev helped John find a comfortable position in the bed.

John knew what he wanted from me. He told me that he knew that he didn't have long to live, that he was dying, and that he was at peace both with the fact that he would die, and with God.

He began to tell the story of his family, beginning with those who were farmers and miners in England before one of them moved to Australia in the 1850s seeking a fortune in the gold fields. I knew that sometimes a person needs to tell the story of his life as a way of integrating his identity, and thus be able to live his dying. Since I had nowhere else that I had to be, I sat back to listen. John spoke very deliberately and particularly about his family history beginning in the 1850s. He told me that after the gold ran out his great grandfather borrowed money and bought acreage from a government land sale in northern Victoria. He spoke of how they lived in tents and how the first thing they built on their land was a church, then a small rural school, and only after church and school were built did they build houses on the farm. There seemed something deeply symbolic in this story: John's values were planted in the story of the family farm: faith, education, family, and farming.

His dad went to that small school, won a scholarship to a private school in the city, then went on to university, and ultimately to a fascinating role as director of the National and Parliamentary libraries.

Only slowly did John come to naming his own life, and it was obvious that his identity included the stories of the people who had lived before him. He had studied agricultural economics at university and that disciplined thinking permeated the conversation. The years 1956 and 1957 were "poor" years, and 1958, the year he got married, was a better year. John became emotional as he talked of his marriage, calling it "the best decision I ever made."

John had been telling me this story for more than an hour and a half when a doctor came in and asked me if I would leave him with the family. When I came back John wanted to go on, though Bev suggested that he was tired.

John told me that he had told the doctor that he was not afraid of dying, that he was at peace with life and at peace with God.

Given his use of God language and given the metaphor of the family church, I offered to pray. I thanked God for John's life, for its integrity, for his contribution to the society at large (he became director of a national farmers' organization), for life shared with Bev, for the forbears who had shaped him, and I asked that God in the appropriate time would receive him.

When I finished the prayer both Bev and John were in tears. I said that I would visit again. "And it's funny," I said. "When someone is going to be married it is all we can talk about, but when someone's dying few people can acknowledge that. When I come to visit I will acknowledge that you are dying."

I don't think that I have ever sat so patiently, so quietly in a hospital room for so long. And certainly it was a privilege to be invited into, and trusted in such an intimate space. John had asked me there as a priestly person; he wanted me to hear his story and to bless him for the onward journey. I hope that I did that. I hope I did what "old Mr Sullivan" said of his pastor—that he walked him to the pearly gates with his wife.

I visited John and Bev a few more times in hospital. They asked me if I would conduct his funeral. I liked the man. He was intense, focused, and asked questions with honesty and personal integrity.

Some time later, I heard that John was in hospital again, so I rang Bev and talked about what was happening. I asked if "it would be appropriate for me to come to the hospital, with a commitment not to stay too long, and if I get there and it isn't appropriate to see him that will be ok. . . . I will not be put out," and I set up a time to visit when Bev would be there.

As I walked up to the ward I wondered about the conversation. Bev had told me that John would not be coming home again. I thought about how we could talk about his death together, and whether or not it would be appropriate to offer to bless John.

When I went in, John appeared comfortable and alert. He was on regular morphine that took away the pain, and there were times when it was difficult for him to breathe. We made small talk for a time. I looked at the photos of a family wedding he had been able to attend a couple of weeks before and we talked about some other large photographs that his sister-in-law had stuck to the wall at the foot of his bed. The photographs were a fantastic vision of the landscape that for so many years had been the family farm, "John and Bev's land." John had also asked me if I had the piece of paper on which he had written a summary of his life. Yes, I had and I told him that it was very impressive. I was particularly struck that he was able to leave the Farmers' Federation with investments of fifty million dollars. He spoke of how it was just a little thing, but he wanted to leave everything in which he had been involved with something that would make a continuing contribution after he had gone. I couldn't help thinking this was a metaphor for how he would leave Bev and his family.

I had a purpose for being there and had questions that I wanted to ask. John was so straight with me. "I have a terminal cancer," he said. "I will not be going home." "Do you have an image of death?" I asked. With the personal integrity that I had come to admire he began to answer the question.

There we were, the three of us together in a hospital room, talking about John's view of his imminent death. In the middle of this very intimate conversation two nurses abruptly pushed open the door. They had jobs to do, things to record, morphine to give. They brought a lot of bustle and noise into the room and they changed the level of the conversation immediately. Once I'd have been flustered by that. This day it was just a matter of them doing their job; when they had left, when the morphine pump was ready to go again, I returned to the moment and refocused the conversation.

I said something like, "John, I asked you about your vision of death and with the integrity that I have come to admire in you, you were telling me that you didn't have a vision of death, that it had been your practice to live responsibly in the present always looking for a positive reading of the things happening to you and around you. You were saying that you had to live the experience of the moment, allowing it to come to you and that you have not yet found an image of death." That was enough to refocus the conversation and we were able to move on. In time, I suggested to John that an image of death might be like in the photographs at the end of the bed: the landscape stretches out towards the horizon. The horizon is not clear; it fades away. Death might simply be like walking towards the horizon."

As the conversation moved to a close John said to me, "I have taken people in your role for granted through my life. Now I realize just how important a role you have and I am grateful for it." I was moved by his acknowledgement.

I said that I had promised Bev that I wouldn't stay too long and that it was time to go. I looked at John and asked if I could bless him. "Yes, please," he said, and held out his hand. I took it and held it and began: "The Lord bless you and keep you..." Afterwards I wondered why I hadn't invited Bev to hold hands with us while I did that, for when I finished the blessing Bev was in tears. She walked with me to the door and put her arm around my back. The need to touch and be touched is strong.

I went to the hospital yesterday. I had two people to visit. Jim was in intensive care. He was in pain, very uncomfortable. I was happy to be quietly beside his bed but he seemed to feel obliged to make conversation with me. I didn't think my visit was helping, so I quietly said, "God be with you. I'm going to take my leave now," to which he responded, "Yeah, he is. I wouldn't survive this without him." And I left.

I walked up the stairs to see John and Bev. I had rung Bev in the morning saying that I would call in. Bev saw me peering in through the window on the closed door and came out to greet me. John was sitting in a chair, shaving. They motioned me to sit down. We talked about general things—like shaving and beards, as you do to be present to a conversation. I mentioned how I had calculated that I had saved two weeks of my life by not shaving, but perhaps John used the time to reflect on his own identity. It was a pretty weak joke. He said no, he used the time for meditation and contemplation. I asked if he had a practice of meditation. He had and we talked about that.

Watching John shave and listening to him talk about his practice of meditation reminded me of my dad, who had died nine years before that. All sorts of things about my dad came to mind, such as how he meditated on colors and how he used to perceive himself to be outside of his body looking down on himself. I knew that I had to be clear that I was here for John and Bev. It would not be appropriate to bring my dad into this conversation even though he was so clearly in my mind. I thought how my own practices of meditation were similar to John's; we both liked to walk while we meditated. I asked Bev if she meditated. No, she said, I am a "doer." Remembering our last conversation when we talked about her hard-edged abstract paintings, I suggested that her painting had probably been a time of meditation for her, to which she agreed

Bev had mentioned on the phone that John did not seem to want to let go of life and die. Now with me in the room as an ally she began to say to John, "The trouble is you will not let go." He listened and said, "I know that you have all given me permission to die. You have been clear that it is ok to let go." And now I knew we were at the edge of the most profound question: How do you die? I remembered my dad asking me, "Douglas, do you know how to die?" and my response: "You have been close enough to death a few times to know about it. When the time comes you will know how to die." With John and Bev, I was sharing a most intimate conversation. I could hear Bev's agitation that this process had been going on too long, and she was becoming frustrated. I could also hear and acknowledge the incredible openness of this conversation. I told them that the quality of their being together in this moment had taken years of building a good relationship. You can't come to a conversation like this without having worked really hard at being open in your relating. I also said that I had been very impressed by the way in which John had lived his life fully, with integrity and responsibility; it was obvious that he had loved life, and you can't just let go of life when you have loved it that much. And I talked about the difference between this and other times in his life when he had been ill and the expectation then that he would get better. Now it is different. Now he is in hospital, knowing that he has a terminal illness, knowing that there is no possibility that he will get better, knowing that he will die. Inside me I was thinking how difficult it must be to wait for your own death, how difficult to wait for your partner's death. And though now Bev was encouraging John to be willing to let go and die, I thought in a week or two, when you are at home alone, Bev, and have time on your hands you will probably regret your impatience in this time. That, of course, was a thought not to be spoken.

John looked quietly across the room and brought our attention to a beautiful deep pink rose beside his bed; he wanted us to notice the beauty of the rose. It had been brought in by a neighbor and was named "friendship." Perhaps he was telling us how beautiful life is, in all its fullness. I wondered at this strange boundary between life and death. You can be terminally ill, on morphine to alleviate the pain, waiting with uncertainty and faith for the moment that is death, and yet still be fully alive in that you can recognize the beauty of the things that are around you.

I offered to pray with them. They hadn't been worshipping people. I chose to pray in general terms, to address God in universal terms. "God thank you for the life that you give us. Thank you for the life that John and Bev have been able to share together over so many years. Thank you for the intimacy and peace that they share. When it is appropriate, in the fullness of your time, open your arms and receive John. Give him peace. Be with Bev and the other members of the family so they may experience peace and strength through this time. Amen." There was a silence, a deep silence. Then they said almost in unison, "What a beautiful prayer."

And still they wait.

I left wondering at the intimacy into which I had been invited. Wondering at the quality of being that Bev and John brought to the moment. Wondering about being welcomed into another's space.

BLOKES' SHEDS

I had been to Jack's place before to visit his studio and to talk about painting, writing, and life in general. Yesterday morning, I walked, as I had on previous visits, towards the front door. There was a handwritten sign stuck to the door pointing me to the side path. I followed the signs around the side of the house and in through the back door to Jack's studio. About twenty blokes from the church were squeezed in, sitting on chairs, and the less lucky ones were on the floor. I was one of the less lucky ones.

Jack had an almost completed painting on his big easel and a number of other works hanging on or stacked against the walls. Normally this was a quiet spot, designed to get the light and to be away from the activity of the house. Jack had some comfortable chairs in the studio, for, as he would tell us, he is learning (at eighty-three) to look longer and paint less. His is also one of the tidiest, cleanest studios I have ever seen, certainly a radical contrast to the chaos in which I paint. Perhaps that is also reflected in the different things we achieve when we paint.

Jack was invited to tell us about his painting: about the work on the easel, how he went about it, what he wanted to achieve, how he sold work, who bought it, where it was hung. Eventually the conversation moved to how he had begun painting, how he had learned the craft and how it shapes him. Barry was the organizer of the day and he cleverly focused the conversation. "Jack you are also a writer and a speaker, tell us about your life from the beginning. How did you get from there to here?" Gently and openly Jack spoke of his life: being one of nine children, having a dad who was a professional athlete, his first job to which he rode his bike sixteen miles each way, summer and winter "for five bob in wages." He spoke of his apprenticeship as a tailor, leaving home to follow his work at sixteen, building a retail business in a country town, and changes in credit laws that made it difficult to earn an income. His shift into the insurance industry—someone had come to him and said, "We think you'd be good at selling insurance"—then into management, and finally on to the inspirational speaking circuit.

The other blokes listened and engaged Jack with interest. One said to me as we left, "I've sat in church with him for years, but never knew about all that." That was my experience when I had sat in the congregation while I was a seminary professor rather than a pastor. I felt frustrated because I knew so little about the lives of the people with whom I worshipped. In this "bloke's shed" we were learning about his life through his interest and his competence.

As we left Jack gave each of us a copy of one of his books: *One Life to Live*.[1]

We went on to Andrew's place. He had just retired as an engineer. He makes model steam trains from scratch. A well-equipped workroom, beautifully and carefully crafted trains, and a two-inch line running around his back garden left us in awe. I wondered again at how easy it is for people to tell you about themselves when you are interested in their competence.

We went together to a club for lunch. How easy, how comfortable is lunch with a group of men when they have shared their competence with their colleagues. And I came home again thinking how lucky I am: I had

---

1. Collis, *One Life*.

had this really interesting morning with twenty men from my congregation, not trying to push my presence on the group, just being one of them. When Sunday morning comes they will know that I know them, and they will expect that I will in turn share my particular competence by leading quality worship for them.

And the name, "Blokes' Sheds"? I had had this fantasy for some time that a really interesting fund raiser would be to offer a tour of bloke's sheds on a Saturday morning. Include breakfast and charge a fee. I'd thought, every bloke likes to see inside other blokes' sheds. I shared the idea with Barry and he changed it in most significant ways. Don't charge. Make it mid-week since most of the men in our congregation are retired. Give men a chance to name who they are by asking them to show and tell about their interest or hobby. And eat lunch together in a pub. That was it.

CHOOSING LIFE OR CHOOSING DEATH

A friend of a friend faced some tough stuff. Stuff that left him feeling so shamed that the only route he could see out was to take his own life. Suicide: what a frightening word it is. Fortunately, at the edge of the abyss he pulled back, opened the door of the car in which he planned to gas himself, and got out.

I was asked, and agreed, to have lunch with these two men the day after.

Preparing for a conversation like that is hard work. I rehearsed a bit of what I knew about people taking their own lives. First, I think about our niece Susan, who suffered from schizophrenia; she listened to the voices in her head, lay down in a vulnerable place, and was killed. A few other people come to mind, not necessarily because I knew them, but because I knew the people they left behind. And I thought of two frightening times in my own life. The first was when I was returning from holiday with my young family and suddenly and irrationally had the urge to pull the wheel of the car so that we would collide with the oncoming traffic.

It required a physical act of the will to hold the wheel steady. The incident scared me and I talked about it in the community of which I was a part at the time.

The other time was similar. I was in a tough time in ministry, required by church rules to end a ministry that I loved. I had talked to a number of congregations who were not interested in me and now I had to talk to a congregation where I had little interest in going. I had to leave one meeting and drive thirty miles to a meeting I didn't want to be at. I stood between the cars waiting to cross a busy road. A huge truck thundered towards me. I felt a physical force on my shoulder pushing me in front of the big truck. I had to physically fight to hold my ground. I was frightened by the suddenness of the urge. Ever since, I've been warily alert to this part of my being. What would I do with this knowledge in a conversation with someone who twenty-four hours previously had meticulously planned how he could kill himself? I knew that I would be present and listen.

A couple of days before that, I had purchased a DVD on musical improvisation by my favorite jazz pianist, Keith Jarrett. The other members of Jarrett's trio (Gary Peacock and Jack De Johnette) talked about why both Keith Jarrett and Miles Davis were such great improvisers. In both cases, they were clear that it was because each had the capacity to listen and hear with all his being. They could both hear so well that they knew how to respond in the fraction of a second available to them.

Being in this conversation was going to be similar. I had practiced and practiced conversation. I had reflected on life and death and suicide. I had experienced glimpses of that same yearning to end it all. I was not in totally unfamiliar territory.

So I joined the conversation with no plans other than to be present. I had suggested lunch in a pub to make the place and the conversation normal. We shared a beer and a meal, and in time Michael began to talk about what had happened. The details don't matter. He told the story, embarrassed that he might be repeating himself. I suggested that there are some stories we need to tell many times as a way of integrating what happened and that he would know when he was storied out. So he told the story, and we others listened. No answers. No criticisms. No sermons. Simply our presence and our attention.

At one point I asked about the shame that would drive him to this, and at another I asked what was happening that he chose to open the door and get out.

After listening for a long time, and when I judged that my sharing some of my experience would contribute something helpful, I told my stories. Michael said, "That is so important to me, to know that I am not the only one who has experienced this."

It was interesting in that we were talking after the event, after he had got to the edge of the abyss and had chosen to turn back, chosen to live. In an instant he saw the futility of his action, and became aware of his wife, his family, and his friends and opened the door of the car and got out. He had chosen to live.

I was reminded of the Moses story in which the people are about to enter the Promised Land. They are told: Today you are to cross the river Jordan and to enter the Promised Land. I am not coming with you. You can choose life or you can choose death, and I say to you: choose life. Michael had clearly and intentionally chosen life.

I offered to Michael that I'd be available to have a lunch or coffee with him every week and that I'd ask him directly, "Have you thought of killing yourself lately?," and that I'd tell him when I thought that what he was saying was bullshit. He was keen that his wife be a part of the conversation and I was happy for that to happen. "I'll still ask those questions, though," I said.

To be sixty-three and have such a life-shaping crisis demands the deepest choice to live. Nothing could be more salutary. How would it reshape Michael's marriage and his relationship with his children and grandchildren and friends? Not only would he have to reshape his life goals, his decision to choose life also needed to be honored and celebrated.

Perhaps what I will remember most about all this is that Michael and his wife had to make an uncertain and perilous journey. The journey was important in resolving the crisis that they faced and it was not going to be easy. They were both very vulnerable, so I invited them to my office with their friend, who was an elder of the congregation, and offered that we share bread and wine, a symbol of God's presence with them as they traveled. So that is what we did: four of us around a coffee table sharing bread and wine, the nourishment of God for a most uncertain journey. Afterwards, Michael commented, "That was the most meaningful communion that I have ever shared in. Thank you."

WORKING OR NOT?

One of the really hard things for me in returning to parish life is to know when I'm working and when I'm not working. When I was minister in other parishes we had an office and I often went there at nine in the morning and would work alongside other people. Now that I live outside the parish, I begin my day in my study/studio at about 8 a.m. I sit quietly and reflectively, writing in my journal, I answer e-mails, and read and think about the Sunday sermon. And I make telephone calls to connect with the people. Then when the peak hour traffic has gone, I drive the twenty-five kilometers to St. Ives, where I have an office in the church. Yesterday I went to visit a couple in their home; then I met with someone at the church office. At lunchtime I went down the street to be in the market place; I took something to read and walked around hoping that I might bump into people from the church. I didn't. So by 2:30 p.m. I headed for home.

I sat in the car and read the Bible passage for Sunday's sermon before I began the drive home. I use the time in the car to prepare for worship.

When I got home I read the passage again, then changed my clothes and went for an hour-long exercise walk. I anguish, even at this stage in my life, as to whether I am working when I go for a walk in the middle of the day. I've always rationalized that ministry needs thinking time. But I know that people who work set hours have to do their exercise either before or after work. So am I working or not working? Am I working at 2 a.m. on a Sunday morning when I wake up thinking about the sermon, trying to work out what and how to say to make it relevant to the lives of the people: am I working then?

I read the lesson and set out on my walk. I headed off down hill to cross the creek behind the school and then made my way up the long hill that is North Rocks Road. I began the walk with a mantra, "Jesus Christ, Son of God and Savior, have mercy on me." I said it over and over, finding a rhythm between my walking, my breathing, and the words of the mantra. Pretty soon I found myself trying to recall the story of the lessons that I'd just read. The lesson for Sunday was Exodus 3:1–6, the story of Moses and the burning bush. I had already decided that I wanted to tell the longer story from Exodus 1:1 through 3:6 because it makes us hear the encounter with the burning bush quite differently. So as I walked I recalled the whole story and rehearsed it as a story. The story, as I was recalling it, seemed too long; it seemed to have too many incidents or chapters to have as one story in worship. But I let the story be in me. Often and quite unconsciously I find myself speaking the story out loud. I cut across the ravine where the Darling Mills Creek had once again fallen back to a trickle after a number of days of heavy rain.

Is this work or not work, I wonder? I always want to justify it as work, but on my bad days, when I'm not confident about who I am, I wonder whether the people in my parish who do other sorts of jobs would consider it to be work. I know they want to be nourished in their faith when they come to worship on Sunday morning, I know they want me to prepare well, and I know that they trust me. But can I really justify a long walk or bike ride in the midday sunshine as work? I do. And I am a little bit more confident that I will have an appropriate sermon to share with the people on Sunday.

BAPTISM

Pastoral ministry in the new parish had been mostly about the pain of people—choosing between life and death, people dying, funeral services, and lament. What joyous relief when Jane and Philip wanted to have their new child baptized!

I went to sit in the local shopping center to have lunch and to write. I like being in public spaces, being visible in the community, even if few people know who I am.

I was preparing for my first baptism in the parish. That night I would be going with an elder to visit the family. I don't like going out at night but it was the only time we could visit when the father would be home and it was important for me that he be a participant in the conversation.

Before such visits it's important for me to think into the visit and to reflect upon what I hope to happen in the conversation. I have always valued the possibility of being engaged with families in the life cycle events of birth, marriage, and death. So when I saw a car last week with an advertisement on it for a civil celebrant of key life cycle events, I felt sad that many people in the wider community no longer know that the church has been addressing such existential questions for a very long time.

It is easy for ministers and priestly persons to get caught up in giving people permission to be angry with God in the face of illness, suffering, and death. It is easy to get caught in the cry of lament. I want also to be able to acknowledge the joy of birth and the song of praise that rises from the depths, to express the joy of the miracle that brings the gift of new life.

I have often thought that we in the church have pushed people away because they don't have the right language to express their praise. We want them to know and name an integrated theology of infant baptism and they want us to hear their sense of being close to God the Creator in expressing the joy they have in their newborn child. I believe that when people bring their infant children for baptism there is a joining of two or more desires: a ritual celebration to mark the birth of the child, and a deep request for the blessing of God on the child and that child's incorporation into the Christian community. Early in my ministry when I "prepared" people for the baptism of their child I wanted them to intellectually "understand" what was happening. I've changed. I have learned to trust the power of the symbol, the power of the act of pouring water on the child's head, the power of the act of marking the cross on the child's forehead, the power of the act of the parents in presenting their child at the front of the church for baptism, to trust the integrity of their response to the question: What do you ask of God's church for your child? "That he/she be baptized into . . ." I have learned to value that which happens when the parents symbolically release their child to the arms of the elder who then introduces the child to the congregation, and to hear the sung blessing when the congregation with one voice calls the blessing of God on the child.

Many in my tradition will say, "But we see so many bring their children for baptism, and afterwards we never see them again." I assume that the children are held in the grace of God nonetheless and always bring to mind a friend who said when he returned to the church after the painful breakup of his marriage, "It was my baptism that held me, and brought me back."

So is the visit I am about to make with the family really about catechesis, checking up on what the people know about the belief, or is it perhaps an act of care, to teach and nourish the parents in the journey of parenting?

We went to visit. Philip and Jane seemed intent on getting to the serious conversation. I tried to affirm the importance of their decision to have

Jordon baptized. In the conversation I was working my way through a mental template of the baptismal service, seeking to interpret to them what I understood would happen when we baptized their son, Jordon.

A couple of days later there were books and cups and bits of paper piling up around my computer as I tried to think into a sermon for Sunday about birth and baptism and blessing. I have in the past struggled to find a theological text that reflects on the birth of a human being. It seems that we Christians are comfortable asking the hard questions about death; we know about the cry from the depths. I can find little that attends to that other song from the depths, the song that praises the Lord of creation for the mystery that brings life in birth, the exultant yell that sings praise for the joy of the new being.

I thought at the time that I would offer a commentary on the baptism service: its questions, processes, and symbols. It could be a way of educating the people about what baptism means, and of teaching them what we are doing at various moments in the liturgy.

1. The question to Philip and Jane, the parents of Jordon who was being baptized: "What do you ask of God's church for Jordon?" "We ask that he be baptized . . ." That answer shows an intention on the part of the parents.

    "Do you believe that the Gospel enables us to turn from the darkness of evil and to walk in the light of Christ?" This is a really tough question. For years it has caused me all sorts of discomfort; I wondered what people might think of us talking about "the darkness of evil."

    In two or three liturgies for the baptism service I have seen recently, this question has been edited, softened, changed. I see it as increasingly important that we acknowledge that there is evil in our world. It is our role as church to name the evil that we see (and not pretend that it is an odd notion). We see wars, bombings of civilians, the destruction of residences. We see torture and killing. There are senseless murders in our streets. We see and make our money on markets that are driven by the notions of highest profit, and we ask few questions about what the markets are doing to people. There is a dark evil present in our world. So I suggest that in the baptism service when we ask this question, we are asking the parents "Do you really want to bring our children into a world like this?" We, of the Christian community, are committed to the view that the Gospel enables us to turn from the darkness of evil and to walk in the light of Christ.

There is more to this. For evil is subtle, incremental, and insidious and it comes in the industrial relations laws that the government is setting up and it comes in the escalating auction for the law and order vote by campaigning political leaders. That is the world into which our children will grow. We in the church have to offer more.

2   In the baptism service I touch the ears and mouth of the child being baptized (in this case, Jordon) and I say: "May the Lord open your ears to hear his word and your mouth to proclaim his praise." What a privilege it is to do this. It reflects our desire that this child will grow to hear and speak of God's grace in the world.

3   When we say the creed together I want to point out that this action of reciting a statement of belief together always requires a compromise of personal belief in order that we might stand together as community. If we have any intellectual rigor, we will always be asking questions about statements of belief that make it difficult to adhere to everything within it, and yet it remains important that we stand and say the creeds together. We compromise something of our individuality to be part of the community.

4   Baptism with water . . . Like the waters of birth, the waters of cleansing . . . There is something in the symbol about dying to the old self and being born into the new, in the name of the triune God.

5   Marking the sign of the cross . . . "Jordon, from this day forward the sign of the cross is upon you and you are engaged to be Christ's disciple."

6   I, as minister, ask the parents to release their child (Jordon) to the elder, and the elder introduces the child to the congregation. Releasing a child into such a vulnerable world is difficult, and

this action is symbolic of that; Jordon is released into God's community with a sense of trust that the community will work with the parents to make his life both safe and blessed.

7   The community sings a blessing as the child is carried among them. What we are saying together is that what we want for this child is that he be held close and blessed by God; in other words, we want the very best (of God) for him in his life. Implicit is that we as people of faith will work to create the sort of world in which that blessing might be fulfilled. The child is returned to the parents who have primary responsibility for his life.

8   The baptism has been conducted as an unconditional act that shares the grace of God. The parents are now asked, in the light of God's grace, to answer some questions that reflect that intentionality in parenting.

9   The congregation commits itself to provide a space where this child and all children among us may be nurtured and grow in faith. This commitment makes us as the community responsible for creating an environment in which children are welcome and can be nurtured and grow in faith. It connects the family and the community in being responsible for creating the space where Jackson can grow in faith.

10 Jordon's parents are given a candle on his behalf and encouraged to light it on anniversaries of this day, with the accompanying words, "Jordon, receive the light of Christ. May you experience Christ's light through your life and walk as a child of the light. Let your light so shine before the world that all may see your good works and give glory to our Father who is in heaven (Matthew 5:16).

RESURRECTION

One of the chaplains, who ministered to the aged and who was in the group that I was leading, seemed too confident about the resurrection, specifically in his firm belief in life after death. That might not have been exactly what he was saying, but it was what I was hearing. As an invited leader, I wanted to push the chaplains in the group to think harder and more openly about resurrection in connection with the lived experience of the people in their care. They were all chaplains working in aged care institutions with people who were in the dying stage of their living. I told how after Easter I had preached a sermon where I wanted to live what I had promised the congregation at my call: that I would live honestly, openly, and deeply as a spiritual leader. So I preached a sermon attempting to name what I understood about resurrection.

I had said on that day that I was uncertain about whether there was life after death. I was uncertain whether resurrection meant that I would see my mum who had died when I was seven and whether she would be in her thirty-five-year-old body before or after her sickness. I was uncertain about whether, like in (English artist) Stanley Spencer's wonderful paintings, people would be pushing up the gravestones dressed in their Sunday best. I was uncertain as to whether I would spend eternity in heaven or what heaven was. I chose to live my life responsibly in the present, to live now in response to the call of Jesus, and to let the future take care of itself. And the funny thing is I said that despite this uncertainty I love the yearly lectionary cycle that brings me in touch with these stories of resurrection, because whether they are literally true or not they have a truth that sustains my living and enables me to live as a person of hope. The resurrection stories demand of me that I live my life responsibly in the present and that I trust God to take care of what happens after my death.

I told the chaplains how a larger than normal number of people sought me individually after church to thank me for the sermon and to tell me, "that was what they believed." Mostly they kept it quiet, compromised the integrity of their belief in order to be part of the community. This day they could be honest.

At the end of the group session one of the chaplains said that he would like to have a further conversation with me about resurrection. He thought the stories true and that they should be acknowledged as true. He wasn't meaning a scientifically verifiable truth, but true nonetheless. We were much closer to agreement than he thought.

The next morning I was conducting a funeral and wondering what I was going to say as "witness to the resurrection." I had some ideas, I had thought about it, and I have been becoming "more conversational" in what I do in funerals. I had encouraged the members of this particular family to speak of their father and grandfather. The son spoke wonderfully, recalling his dad's early life, giving context and color. As he concluded he spoke of his father's having been a scout master and a very organized person. His dad had arranged for his ashes to be placed in a memorial wall alongside his wife's. And he had written the inscription that he thought should go in the wall. Lots of words, but at the bottom a scouting symbol: a circle with a dot in the centre of it, meaning "I have gone home." It was a profound note for the son to find, and to be able to read at this point.

Then the husband of a granddaughter spoke in ways that honored the soul of the man. As he concluded, he told of those last days when the grandfather had called out the name of his daughter who had died three years ago. Something like, "I'm not ready yet, but I will be ready soon." I had a quiet smile. I've heard stories like that before and they contain something that is "true" about the transition from life to death, and is spoken of in such a wonderful metaphor. Then the grandson-in-law spoke of how he imagined that on Saturday evening his wife and his daughter (both of whom had died before him) had come (to the hospital room) to collect their husband and father. "It is not scientifically provable," he said, "but belief is different from truth, and I know what I believe."

I sat there thinking on what I was to say as "witness to the resurrection" and wondering if any words at all were necessary from me as the minister. These people had said it all. They had told the story of the life of their dad and granddad in a meaningful way. They had acknowledged his soul, and they had named their belief in the resurrection.

I spoke briefly, wanting simply to affirm what had been spoken. I affirmed that at ninety-one, when both body and mind are tired, death is appropriate. The important text became the family's own words: the circle with the dot in the middle of it, "I have gone home" and the story of the daughter who had already died being present in the room with her dad, and the beautiful interpretive comment, "truth is one thing and belief another. I know what I believe." I repeated the words of John 14: "In my father's house are many rooms . . ." They needed no further explanation. It was so obvious that what nourished and sustained the life of the mourners was their belief in the resurrection.

A DIFFICULT SERMON TO PREACH AND A BLANK MIND

Ministry changes pace and gears so often that it is difficult to keep up. A funeral during the week for a group of people not necessarily part of Sunday's worshipping community. And a worship service that addresses different questions for a different group of people. That is how it was this week; I had to be alert, open to the very different needs of the people at worship. The words had to speak into their lives in relevant ways.

The National Council of Churches had nominated this Sunday as Refugee Sunday—an important and politically contentious issue in Australia as it is in many of our countries. I had done a lot of research on the subject of refugees and worked hard to think what would be the best way to present the material so that it could be relevant for the lives of the people. I woke at 6 a.m. and lay in bed trying to rehearse the sermon—and I was absolutely blank. I got up and wrote four pages of notes but still could not see how I was going to preach this sermon in any coherent and meaningful way. Driving to church I rehearsed it in my mind again and still it wasn't clear. I was going to have to trust that when I stood up to speak I would find the words because I had done the research and the thinking and praying necessary to preach.

The choir sang so beautifully, "I have one life to live." Then I stood to preach. How to begin? What to say? Acknowledging the special contribution of the choir would enable the people to move from their prayer to the sermon, and it would help me to connect with them. Then I was into what I wanted to say.

Facing the congregation without any notes means that I have to talk to the people, and I pick up lots of clues from them about how they are responding. I began to find my way forward, the people listening with intent. I didn't want to tell them what to think, but to give them information about a most complex human predicament and to help them understand that we have first to attend to the lived experience of others, then to hold that in dialogue with the received tradition of faith to shape an ethic and practice of care and justice. To encourage people to be thoughtful and proactive about the sort of nation they want our nation to be is part of my calling, and part of the call of all Christians.

After worship ever so many people thanked me for the sermon. It was brave, spot on, timely, helpful, and challenging, the people said. Some came with tears, to tell me stories of their family's journeys from Europe immediately post World War II, others to reflect with discipline on the complexity of world and regional politics and to share their concern for appropriate and careful action. I became intrigued afterwards thinking how on the one other occasion that I chose to be open about a very difficult and controversial topic the people were similarly responsive. It excites me that the people want to think hard about faith and life, and that they want help to do that.

5

Being a Theological Interpreter

MINISTERS BECOME THEOLOGICAL INTERPRETERS in many settings. Part of the role of being a spiritual leader is to help others discern something of the voice of God in difficult times and places. Darkness comes in all sorts of ways, even in a confusing breakfast.

AFTER A CONFUSING BREAKFAST

Being a theological interpreter involves helping the people of our community listen to what the artists in our community are saying. It can involve more than that and there are times when the people are confused about important issues about what it is they believe and how that belief shapes them. In a multicultural and multifaith society, understanding the relationship between Islam and Christianity involved me as theological interpreter.

On Saturday morning, a week ago, I went with a number of my parishioners to an ecumenical breakfast. In our region there is a very strong commitment to ecumenicity on the part of the lay people and they meet for three or four key activities during the year, typically a breakfast, a lunch, and a dinner each with a speaker. The clergy tend to stay away. Last week the speaker was a Presbyterian. The speaker had grown up in Egypt and his role in the Presbyterian Church is to focus the church's evangelism on Muslim peoples. He spoke as one who, in his own words, "loves Muslim people, but hates Islam." He spoke in a way that was aggressive, inflammatory, disturbing, and that created and fed prejudices. Some of the things that he said were similar to what was said by Protestants about Catholics forty years ago.

I went away wondering. As I listened to my people, I heard their distress. Somewhere inside them they knew that what had been spoken was unhelpful, but they would have been pushed to say why. Perhaps they didn't have the skills to think critically about the spoken word or poorly exegeted texts.

I resolved to make my Sunday reflection a response to what I had heard. I would seek to understand something about the relationship between Christians and Muslims in the present. An e-mail came from one of the people who had been at the breakfast suggesting it would be good if I could make passing comment. I began to read and think. I knew next to nothing about Islam, nothing about Muslim peoples and their practice, and even less about Mohammed and how he received the revelation that is the Qu'ran. After a good bit of reading I wondered if there is any difference between the way Mohammed received his recitation and Mozart received his music . . . and even if Charles and John Wesley's body of hymns is a later revelatory voice added to the Christian tradition by being added to the hymnody.

As I began to read and think about the things that had happened at breakfast, the issue became bigger and bigger until, when I stood in front of the people to "preach," I said, by way of opening, that it was the most important sermon or reflection I had made since being minister of this congregation. In the morning paper had appeared two stories, one of a political leaflet for the forthcoming election that denigrated Muslims, criticizing a federal government initiative to integrate Muslim people and then an inciting remark: "many Lebanese thugs (in the Cronulla riots) were the product of incest and . . . these bloodlines had led to an underclass of Islamic supremacists," and the U.S. vice president Dick Cheney had been here describing the "terrorists'" ultimate aim to establish a caliphate covering the region from Spain, across North Africa, through the middle East and South Asia all the way to Indonesia—"and it won't stop there." Mr. Cheney had said that if the jihadists tasted victory in Iraq they would look for new missions.[1] I did not try to represent Islam or say why Christianity was different, but to give people resources for living well with difference.

I wanted to speak about how we attend to and listen to people who are different from us. In this case, how do we and how will we listen to Islam? How do we listen to people who are Muslims? How do we get past the fear factor? How might our community be given the tools to think critically about what had been said at Saturday's breakfast?

It is an extraordinarily complex issue that goes to Middle East geography, politics, markets, culture, and religion over hundreds of years, and

---

1. *Sydney Morning Herald,* 24 February 2007, 1.

those tensions are carried around the world with migration and made far more complex with the attacks on New York City and Washington D.C. on September 11, 2001. It is ultimately about world peace.

As I thought about this through the week, I wondered: had I been a young person in Germany in the 1930s, what I might have learned and thought about the Jews and what might have been my reaction to what the state was doing? Could we possibly be going down a similar path, forgetting our history so quickly?

I reflected on many important things that morning, but always prodding at me, as in every sermon, was the question: where is the gospel in this? How might I say, "Thus says the Lord?" Or, how could I say to the people, "Herein is hope," since they have come intentionally to worship God? The speaker at the breakfast had begun by quoting from John 14: "Jesus said I am the way, the truth, and the life, no one comes to the Father, but by me." That seemed to be drawing a line on the ground that would shape a conflictual relationship. It assumed a universal authority for a statement that may only have authority for those who have come to claim it as authority. How different might the presentation have been, how different might our relations with those who are different be if we chose to begin with a different statement of Jesus, say the words of the sermon on the plain (Luke 6:27–36): "Love your enemies, do good to those who hate you, bless those who curse you, pray for those who abuse you."? I chose to end my reflection by reading these words and hoping that the people would hear them as a guide to how they might live as the people of God in this difficult, fragile, uncertain, and frail world.

The people heard me, and they came each one to thank me. "You spoke on a political issue, but were not political." "You are never boring when you speak. I always am pushed to think about things." "You have made sense of my confusion last Saturday." So many comments, all engaged, all thoughtful, all reflecting the people of God thinking deeply about how to be faithful in a complex world.

The preaching took so much energy. I was so intensely focused, I was still preaching the sermon when I woke up this morning after a long and deep sleep.

CHRIS'S INVITATION TO WRITE ABOUT HIS SHOW

It is not only in overtly theological or religious contexts such as worship or a funeral that a pastor is called on to name the voice of God in the lives and works of those around us. Chris, a friend of recent years, whose wife had recently died all too young of lung cancer, had invited me to write about his work in the catalogue for his show. Though he may not consciously have thought of me this way when he invited me to write this catalogue piece for his exhibition, I was in essence being asked to be a theological interpreter or public theologian.

And so it was that I had gone to Chris Wyatt's home for lunch one Friday recently, bread rolls and ham under my arm. I wanted to look more closely at the paintings he was getting ready for this show. Paintings were spread everywhere throughout his home—I couldn't help but look. So we drank a Guinness and looked. Chris is a slow, deliberate, and thoughtful painter. He seems to contemplate each brush stroke for days weeks, months, and sometimes for years. He works the painting from the inside out. He starts with a few marks on the canvas or board and very slowly builds up the painting. The figures that dominate his work come to solid form quietly and gently. It is like God in Genesis, breathing breath into the clay that becomes Adam. He is a disciplined editor of his own work, spending weeks and months looking at the emerging image and going back to redo what doesn't satisfy his eye and heart. The colors initially feel somber, they do not dominate; rather they work to create the emotional mood of the painting. Often at first appearance the paintings are dark, and the viewer has to experience that darkness before the painting reveals its vibrating, shimmering glow. When Chris paints, the painting is much more than the color you can see.

Chris often works, and reworks, and works again the same theme. I am reminded of a mentor of mine who once wrote to me, "I believe strongly in endless repeated efforts to render the same image like Cézanne or Morandi—that way we go into our deepest being and produce what no other artist can." That is what Chris Wyatt does. He goes into his deepest being and produces what no other artist can.

But I digress. I'd been in his home for a few minutes looking and he called me outside to see a couple of works that he had in the garage he uses as a studio. One was gouache, which is a water-based opaque paint. He hauled it outside and leaned it against the fence so that I could see it. The sky threatened rain and I worried out loud that if it rained the painting would be ruined. In response to which Chris told me how he had recently left outside a painting he was particularly pleased with, it rained, and when he found it in the morning it had all been washed away. Never treat your own work as precious, he said.

With the sky threatening rain, Chris went into the back of the studio and dragged out one huge canvas after another. He laid them side by side against the fence over the top of the gouache, one big diptych. He asked me if I had seen this painting before. No, he'd told me about it, but I hadn't seen it. He'd shown it once and had some negative reactions. Yet Terry Cutcliffe, the curator of this new show, wanted it in the show.

I leaned against the wall of the house and looked. The phone rang inside the house and Chris went to answer it. I stayed looking, the rain came, and this big oil painting protected the gouache. I took out a pencil and began to sketch the figures from the oil painting in my book. My heart swelled up in my chest, my breathing became shallow and tight. Somehow I knew that I was in front of one of the great crucifixion paintings. I knew the subject of the painting was Anita Cobby, a twenty-six-year-old nurse and beauty pageant winner who had been raped and murdered in Western Sydney in 1986. Her murder is remembered as one of the most horrifying and violent crimes ever perpetrated in Australia. A cold wind was blowing through me as I looked. I wished that I had brought my coat from the car. But the painting was about more than Anita Cobby's murder, though that specific event and subject gave Chris Wyatt the opportunity to paint an image that is universal. Even if you knew nothing of the story of Anita Cobby you would still be deeply moved by this painting because it is about what it means to be human.

Chris paints the human condition. He demands that the person who looks at his paintings reflect on the dark side of being human, for only if you do this can you be honest about humanity. He paints in such a way that the inherent evil is not out there somewhere in someone else but lying dormant in the one who looks. The threat to the viewer is not so much in what is happening to Anita Cobby, but that I, the viewer, might be involved in the terrible act. It took five or six hundred years before the crucifixion of Jesus appeared in paintings. The act was too offensive. Now the crucifixion image has become trite and banal; people paint crucifixion paintings without much thought, the image is worn as jewelry and asks no questions of the viewer. Chris Wyatt's painting is a genuine crucifixion painting, for it confronts the person willing to give it time with some of the harder questions about being human and it breaks into the depths of their humanness. It recognizes the ability of the strong and powerful to take advantage of the weak and vulnerable. The slow buildup of the paint, the quiet resolution of the painting, the tough mind of the artist asking even tougher questions of society makes this a genuinely prophetic work. You cannot look honestly at this painting without asking hard questions about what it means for us to live responsible lives. This painting is of a life and world turned upside down, and Chris, as artist, is saying to all of us, "Have a look at yourself." You see in his work a seriously thought out worldview that recognizes the moral frailty of the human being.

We went inside and we had lunch. Duke Ellington joined our conversation from the crackling vinyl Chris loves. We talked more about paintings, music, life, and religion.

Prominent in the room was a painting of Catriona, Chris's wife, who had died the previous September. I recalled being part of a dinner party around this table, looking at the portrait that was in the process of being painted at that time, when Catriona said, "Long after I am gone, when people hold up this painting of me, I want you to remember and say that I was a party animal who liked to celebrate life." Chris knew how ill Catriona was, and was describing in paint his emotional response to her illness. He was touching in paint what his words could never reach. That is how he has always painted, observing, reflecting, thinking deeply, using the human figure to say things about life that are way beyond where his words will go; always serious, always thoughtful, and quietly profound.

Chris wrestles in his paintings with the deepest existential questions about what it means to be human.

Some might respond to the darkness in his work with fear. They may walk away disturbed. Sitting quietly over lunch, eating the bread rolls, drinking a beer, talking, the colors begin to vibrate, to shimmer, to glow, and the question of where is the hope in the work begins to emerge. These works are all realistic about life and for that reason are full of hope. The gentle yellows, reds, and ochres come from within the figures and they encompass the figures. It is a gentle warm light, a comfortable blanket that soothes the heart and you know that while moral frailty is real, there is something much more than that that nourishes human existence.

We shared a pot of tea. I kept going back to look again. Then, reluctantly, because I've arranged to meet someone else, I left Chris and his paintings. I got in my car and drove away. Yet the paintings, the images, the texture, the marks, the colors, the brush strokes, and the mood have stayed with me. The paintings are the product of a deeply reflective and hope-filled life.

A MONDAY OFF AND A VISIT TO SEE ANSELM KIEFER'S RECENT WORK

Monday is my day off. Sometimes having a day off when other people are working exacerbates the loneliness of ministry. Heather had made plans to do something with our daughter, Kirsty. I didn't like the idea of spending the day by myself, so I rang an artist friend, Peter, and suggested a trip to the art gallery to see an Anselm Kiefer exhibition. I wanted to do something other than ministry, to be with someone who liked to make paintings, to talk about art and life, and to be stimulated.

The gallery has long shown one or two of Kiefer's earlier works. The first of these is close to the entry to the gallery and we saw it on the way in. In English it is called "faith hope and love." Kiefer often writes the title on the surface of the work in what looks like white chalk. This work has an airplane propeller made from lead projecting forward from canvas that reflects a grey ocean rolling forward its waves. It has about it a sense of Armageddon, the end times of humanity. Peter hadn't known Kiefer's work before and I pointed out this work to him. Awake at night, in the small hours of the morning. I began to understand this painting. Kiefer had been born in Lübeck after the Allied bombing that razed the community and lived there for the early years of his life. The small boy would have heard stories of the raids of thousands of bombers of the Allied Air Forces and he'd have walked in the destruction they had caused.

We rode down the escalator to where one of the gallery's newer acquisitions "hangs." "Hangs" might be a euphemism because this work includes concrete stairs on a canvas coated with cement. One of the gallery guides told us he wanted a hard hat to work near it. It would have needed engineers and machinery to get this work into place in the gallery. I had stood in front of this work previously, on a few occasions. I didn't "understand" it. I just wanted to experience it. I read the notes on the wall and they didn't really help me. A concrete staircase in two pieces, metal construction rods projecting in an untidy way reminiscent of a building, either unfinished in construction or destroyed, were somehow affixed (with welded metal frame) to the front of the canvas. For Peter and I there was a sort of awed silence, a joke about the concrete stairs. Later I came to think of the stairway images in the Bible—of Jacob and his ladder, the vision of Peter in Acts 11 where there was something like a large sheet coming down from heaven—and these images seemed to speak of transcendence; a connection between this world and the world beyond. Later, days later, the question forms: How do we transcend the destruction brought about by evil in our world? How do we ascend or rise above the pain and darkness that destroys life?

We walked into the exhibition. The first work: a pile of cut glass on the floor, each piece with a number written in black ink. And, through the scattered and broken glass, human hair. There was a description of the work on the wall pointing us to some mythological connections. They were unknown to us and didn't readily make sense. But we knew enough about the Holocaust to see in the glass and the hair allusions to the death camps of Nazi Germany, and Pol Pot in Cambodia, and Russia, and Rwanda, and Iraq; and in the sharp edges of the glass, in its fragility, in the numbers, in the randomness, and in the human hair, allusions to evil and sin.

Peter and I went on through the exhibition and sat and talked about it over a roast beef and Camembert roll. After lunch we watched the video taped conversation with the artist. I had imagined him to be big, heavily muscled, rough hands, weathered. On the film he looked my size, my age. He wore a grey suit-coat, a black t-shirt, he was bald, clean shaven, wore glasses. He was articulate in English (not his first language), he was thought-filled, could have been mistaken for a lawyer (in fact he had done his early study in law) or a doctor. He paints these huge works without the help of assistants. I'd love to see a video of him working on a canvas.

Kiefer is to my mind one of the greatest artists in the world at the present. I do not comprehend how a human being has the capacity to conceive and then the technical ability to construct such works. The works themselves become the voice of a "poetic" genius. Sometimes I look at a modern aircraft and think of the miracle that has been its creation. It would not be possible for one human in their lifetime to design and build such a machine from scratch. It takes thousands of people, over generations, working together, building on what others have done—many, many people contributing little bits of knowledge and technical know-how.

I stand in awe of Kiefer's genius, his imaginative ability to conceive the ideas that become his works and the technical genius that allows him to construct them.

Born in Germany in 1945, living his childhood in the midst of a country devastated by massive and continued bombing, his work has always suggested to me that somehow he carried the guilt for the Third Reich. His paintings and constructions have been dark, grey, heavy, leaden, and voicing lament. The material with which he "paints" is so much more than paint: lead, earth, cement, fragile grasses, oil, emulsion, acrylic, sand, glass hair, glue, bitumen, sticks, branches, trees . . . anything he can find that gives voice to the emotion of the questions he asks. And each canvas is inches deep with a temptingly tactile surface. I want to run my hands across it, put my face in it, and feel its physicality as well as seeing it.

In 1991 Kiefer vacated his studio in Germany and moved to France where he has created a huge space and works inside and out, creating a most amazing display of paintings and sculptures. When I look, I become aware of the way in which he physically and conceptually shapes ideas like no other, a technical facility beyond my comprehension, an engagement with the deep stuff of being.

I was looking for a day off. This gallery visit was pushing me to do some of the most intense "reading" about faith and life that I have done in a long time. Two nights later I woke in the middle of the night and, aware of my wife's gentle breathing beside me, I lay in bed for what seemed like hours, happily and vividly recalling each work and thinking on the significance of the whole showing of Kiefer's recent work. In this recent work it seemed to me that he had moved from images of guilt and despair to images of hope and resurrection. I had already decided that I would invite my congregation to a "seminar in the public realm" in which we would meet in the gallery and I would help them to look at this work.

This exhibition of Keifer's Recent Work[2] has as a central motif, a room, entitled "Palm Sunday." Kiefer quotes the Isaiah 45:8 passage—

> "Shower, O heavens from above,
> And let the skies rain down righteousness;
> Let the earth open, that salvation may spring up"
> And let it cause righteousness (justice) to spring up also;
> I, the Lord, have created it."

—that begins the Palm Sunday (and Advent) liturgy. Kiefer recognizes Palm Sunday as the beginning of the epic, archetypal journey of Jesus to his death on the cross and his resurrection. More than anything I have seen of Kiefer's, this later work, has color . . . the transition from lead and concrete to the red soil as the material from which the work is made. And color that comes in a new way— so warm, so encompassing, so gentle, so inviting. There is an openness in the work. And more than anything, hope and new beginning.

---

2. Art Gallery of New South Wales, May 20–July 29, 2007.

On the floor of this room depicting Palm Sunday is a huge palm tree; its roots trimmed, its fronds or branches cut back, and the few that are there have the earthy brown of death in flora. Loose dirt falls from it to the floor. This time the comment on the wall gives me a clue: Like Lazarus and Jesus, there is the question: will this tree live or die? And, somehow, the hope that is in the nature cycle, if it is replanted it will live.

It intrigues me that in the filmed interview Kiefer describes himself as "not Catholic" but he draws on the Palm Sunday entry to Jerusalem story of the Christian tradition to carry the power of what he wants to say.

Henri Matisse had done something similar in the Vence Chapel, when, after a near-death experience of his, the nuns who nursed him asked him to help with the design of their recently burned-out chapel. Matisse wanted to be able to design every part of the chapel, and he drew on the Christian story to create this crowning work, which might, in my view, be the summation of his life's work. So many people speak and have spoken a word that might be seen to be "of God" when they are reaching for a language to help them in the mysterious places that are beyond (normal) speech.

I went back to look again at three of Kiefer's bigger works. They are huge! They're 2.8 meters high and 7.6 meters long!

The first of these works had engaged me through memories of my dad.

When I stood in front of the painting *Die Nachricht vom Fall Trojas* (2006), I could see the landscape that Kiefer has represented so many times, with its furrows all converging on a central point, the scarified land, and below those furrows what looks like barbed wire and skulls and on the surface that is earth and charcoal and dried straw and oil paint is a white line going through what look like towns on a map, each with a Greek name. The white line looks like it documents a path that winds back upon itself a few times. The march my dad was on seemed to go around in circles, just to keep the prisoners moving. So, as I looked at this work I thought of my dad's involvement both with the planes bombing Germany and in the march as a prisoner of war in Germany. There are splatters of black paint on the surface and they look like small explosions going off all over the surface . . . some lively colors too, the ultramarine blue, vermillion, yellow ochre, and rusty browns. Peter thought it could make an unstable person vulnerable to their instability.

I walked through the Palm Sunday section and then to look at the two more colorful works in the final room. What had astounded me about these works was the warm and generous color: pinks and soft orange/ochres breaking forth from the grays. There was a road going into the canvas, bending into the horizon. Initially I thought of Vincent Van Gogh's near to, or, perhaps, last painting. "Crows on the Cornfields" (July 1880). The road disappears into the golden cornfields, the black crows in flight, the impasto-ed blue sky. The structure of the works are similar, maybe the content is similar, but the scale of the Kiefer work, the materiality of the paint and earth and grass, the physical shaping of the surface, the scratching and scraping and throwing and splashing of paint . . . and then the color. There is something in how the physical earth can grow the flowers again and again, there is hope, there is joy in the color, there is life, there is resurrection. Palm Sunday begins a journey that ends in hope. It is transcendent.

Kiefer helps me clarify something of both being a public theologian and a theological interpreter. This is public theology. Not a theology that I as one of the church speak, but a theology that I see in the voice of God breaking through the imagery/poetry of someone in the deep struggle of life. With integrity, Kiefer lives authentically and fully who he is and he creates these works that reflect the imagery of struggle in the prophets and psalms of the Old Testament, but then reaches forward. Whether or not he drew on the language of Palm Sunday, his work reflects a breaking through of something new. These 2006 works are most amazing. What I have tried to do as pastor is to listen to the lives of the people and name when I think the voice of God is breaking through. That is what I think Kiefer does and I think he speaks deep truth when he does it.

And then, another serious thought: Is Anselm Kiefer the Karl Barth of the present? Theologians are no longer writing big systematic theologies. Audre Lorde[3] speaks about "poets giving form to something in order that it can be thought." To my mind, Kiefer's life work is a systematic theology, though he may not see it as such; it is an incredibly thoroughly thought out system of images that break open new understanding of life as well as integrating, and bringing healing.

---

3. Melanie A. May, *A Body Knows*.

So, I'm suggesting that the "new" systematic theologies might be totally in poetic or aesthetic form, that it might come from the life work of an artist whose mind is bigger, and whose grasp of life is not shaped by how something should be thought, nor by footnoting who has thought what along the way; rather the theology will be shaped by the artists who think about the biggest and deepest questions with open and honest discipline. The works Kiefer creates are true in every sense of the word.

I organized a Sunday afternoon visit for my congregation to the gallery to see this exhibition. Twenty braved the cold and rain, and I introduced them to the theology of Kiefer.

WRITING A CATALOGUE PIECE FOR THE BLAKE PRIZE FOR RELIGIOUS ART

I have been thinking about what makes art religious for a long time and was recently asked to write a brief essay for the catalog to the Blake Prize for Contemporary Religious Art, held in Sydney each year. The Blake has been a prestigious major art prize in Australia for nearly sixty years. The prize and accompanying exhibition were particularly significant n the 1950s because the Blake provided the venue for the most contemporary of artistic expressions at a time when other competitions were much more conservative.

One Saturday I went to help receive the entries for the prize—six hundred and fifty of them! Four hundred might be the more usual number. My first reaction was to be awed by the technical competence of the works. But at night I tossed and turned in my bed at what I discerned as the lack of freedom, lack of depth, lack of theological or religious knowing evidenced in the paintings. In its worst forms, people seem to think that if they put a cross or a Buddha in the work that makes it religious.

Yesterday, I went back to help with the judging. Each year there are different judges: one is an artist, one represents arts administration, and the other is a religious person from one of the major religious traditions. Yesterday I helped carry these works of all sizes, weights, and forms before the judges, and I listened as they commented on them. They select about ninety of the six hundred and fifty to hang as finalists and one as the winner. It was a physically exhausting day for me, mentally exhausting for the judges. So many works that it is difficult to view them all with integrity—in fact when you calculate it comes out at about a mere forty seconds per work. Little opportunity for allowing the works to come to you slowly, and for seeing and experiencing the layering in them. The judges who know art know what makes a painting work, and can spot that quickly. The religious judge has to know what makes a "text" religious and often that takes longer. It intrigues me how much the art judges assume about what is "religious" and their reluctance to allow the religious person to know about art. The whole thing is a really interesting exercise. Sometimes there are works that I think are dubious and the judges select them, and other works that I think are most significant the judges reject. The day is a wrestling with the imagination of the society or culture for the revelatory images, images that might in some way reflect the in-breaking voice of God.

We had been carrying works to and fro all day. I was physically spent. Yet there was one big box left, a box that had come from an aboriginal community in North Western Australia, and I had the job of unpacking it. I took sixty screws out of one side of the box only to discover it was the wrong side, and then had to put the sixty screws back, and take out the sixty screws on the other side. I had a big electric drill and it weighed a couple of kilos. My arms were already aching so I had to share the task. When we got the lid off, the painting was wrapped in bubble wrap with a cover over the surface. That required cutting of tape, and eventually we got to the work: a stunning piece by an aboriginal woman (Shirley Purdie from the Warmun Community) from the East Kimberley region, painted in the style of that region using traditional pigments from the earth. The work depicted the Stations of the Cross and her land. It was what the artist called a "two way," reflecting both traditional culture and Christian tradition. We all stood in a tired and awed silence looking at it. I think that we all instantly knew that this was the stand-out piece of the whole lot; that this, the last work that we looked at would be the winner—and it was. It was religious because of its fresh beauty, because of its stillness, because of its appropriate depiction of the Christian tradition, because it would contribute significantly to worship, because it asked and addressed appropriate questions about the nature of being, because it acknowledged the earth of the region from which it came. The work reflected a deep quiet within the soul of the one who had made it, and it reflected an integration of the diverse cultural and religious influences on the artist over all her living.

The previous year I had written the catalogue piece for that competition around the question of what makes a work of art religious. For many years I had wrestled with this question. The theologian Paul Tillich had influenced my thinking considerably and my doctoral work was on Tillich's understanding of expressive art. The question shapes an understanding of revelation within contemporary society. As spiritual leader, priestly person, minister, I am in this case speaking in the public realm, articulating an understanding that can have an impact on how the broader society hears and discerns the active voice of God in the present.

Let me offer some criteria for what might make a work of art religious:

- Does the work link contemporary life with religious tradition to shape meaning and action?
- Does the work reach to address the mystery of "being" that is beyond speech?
- Does it give form to the darkness that surrounds the source of "being"?
- Does the work speak prophetically by asking ultimate questions of the contemporary society?
- If the work were placed alongside traditional religious symbols would it bring those symbols to life in a new way?
- Does the work by its beauty reveal something of the divine?
- Is the work true? Is it true to the disciplined observation of the world by the artist? Is it true to the integrity of the artist? Is it true to the materials used? Is it true to the nature of being? Is it true in its ability to speak deeply to the viewer?
- Does it attempt to depict in fresh ways the stories, symbols, and truths of a religious tradition?
- Does the work have the capacity to break into the emotions and deep places of the viewer in ways that shape "being"?
- And, I might add, does it explore the way light comes out from the darkness?

Art that is religious has integrity. It demands something of the viewer. It allows or enables the "voice of the divine" to break into society in fresh ways. It shapes cultural and individual identity. Art that has this integrity will create a compassionate and caring society. Society always needs a voice that breaks open the important questions in fresh ways; contemporary religious art does that.

THE STATIONS OF THE CROSS PROJECT[4]: WHY THE STATIONS?

Most stories in this book have been written as they happened. The telling of this story about the Stations of the Cross project in which we have asked fifteen major artists each to produce a visual image for a particular Station is central to my journey, central to my finding a new and rewarding direction, central to my finding my way as a theological educator in a more open environment. This project that has been run for two years and now pushes into its third has been a literal reflection of how I have found light in darkness. Because that happens for me I have found that it is happening for the artists and the viewers also. So I have written the story some time after the event and it is a central part of the whole journey of finding light out from darkness.

A few years ago I had gone to an exhibition of the major New Zealand artist Colin McCahon in the Art Gallery of New South Wales. McCahon is considered by some commentators to be the equivalent of the American abstract expressionists. He often painted a graffiti-like text using the Bible for his subject. Early in his life he had seen a graffiti on a rock in the countryside and watched the local sign writer putting up signs in shop windows; this influenced what he painted. Looking at his work is reminiscent of looking at a blackboard in school on which much has been written, erased, and written on again. There is evidence of writing and erasing and writing again. The script varies in size and emphasis. The subject of the text is always secondary to the act of looking at the whole. The surprise when you get to the text is that it is from the New English Bible translation and that it somehow intimately reflects where McCahon was in his life at the time. So when he knew clearly who he was there are the great I

---

4. You can view the images exhibited in the Stations project at www.stives.unitingchurch.org.au. A DVD of the project is available too.

AM paintings and when towards the end of his life he was in despair and depression the text came from Ecclesiastes and was about futility.

He also painted numbers; looking at the paintings took me back to mathematics classes in primary school. I really enjoyed the visual experience of looking at these "number paintings," but I had little clue as to the relevance of the numbers. Then I made a connection. The numbers ranged from one to fourteen. McCahon had painted a series of landscapes each numbered 1 through 14, and there at the base of the paintings in small text was the reference to the St. Francis Stations of the Cross that originated in the thirteenth century.

I had never looked with any interest at the Stations of the Cross before. And now, when I did, the idea grabbed me. I saw the sequence of stations as an existential prayer. The journey of Jesus to his death on the cross was a metaphor for the journey on which we all go in life as we become aware of our own death and mortality. I began to "pray" the Stations. I drew them in my sketchbook, I made my Lenten discipline to paint a series of the Stations. I painted fifteen works each twelve inches by twelve inches. I laid them out on the lounge room floor and looked at them closely. I engaged the questions they asked of me and I opened myself to being shaped in new ways.

In my first year in the St. Ives parish two fellowship groups in the parish invited me to come and address them on any topic that I liked. It was approaching Easter so I got some images of Colin McCahon's work and introduced the people to his art, and then I showed them images of my Stations of the Cross work; I wanted to introduce them to this amazing existential prayer and to open them to new ways of imagining their own faith. I had no idea that this was the beginning of something much bigger for us as a community.

I shared a coffee with a colleague sometime later. I was telling him how I had found the discipline of praying the Stations of the Cross through drawing and painting such a helpful exercise. As we talked, somewhere emerged the idea of inviting major artists each to produce a Station of the Cross for a special Easter exhibition that we would open to a broader public.

For me praying the Stations of the Cross had provided a structured way of finding the light that emerges from the darkness. I saw in the Stations of the Cross a way of acknowledging the lived experience of the people; the people of the church community in St. Ives knew what it was to stumble under the weight of their mortality and to be stripped bare by life itself. They had experienced the deaths of loved ones; they knew the vulnerability of their own frail bodies; it was not always easy to talk about, but it was there. And they were a people for whom it was important to be honest about their lived experience. As I introduced the people to these images I had little idea of just how important the prayer was for me.

I began looking for fifteen artists. I asked some friends who were artists what they thought of the idea. Their responses were positive, encouraging. I determined to call some artists whose reputations I knew, but whom I had never met. The first response I had was what sealed the project: "That sounds like a fun idea, I'll be in that." Before long I had fifteen artists. I put their names in a hat and pulled out a numbered station for each of them. Emerging from my own praying and painting of the stations I was able to write what I have called a "pastorally informed commentary" on the Stations. I gave the commentary to the artists as a beginning point and left them six months to create their work.

As I listened to the congregation, I realized I needed to tell them more about the project. So, I preached a couple of sermons telling them about the traditional stations and how what we were doing was a contemporary take on those.

People came to see the art. It was so exciting for us as a congregation. In the first year, there were 820 visits over four days, in the second year, 1150-plus visits over ten days. When I told one of the artists about the number of visits, he said to me, "The numbers don't matter. The thing is that people asked really important questions about life and were engaged in deep ways."

The questions of mortality and finitude have shaped me for as long as I can remember. Probably the questions began to form when my grandparents died and then took greater root when my mum died, especially around the question, "What happened when my mum died?" Not, "what happened physically?" Not, "why does the heart stop or why does the breathing stop or why does the brain stop?" But a meaning question: "What is the meaning in death?" "What is the effect on the living?" I know there is emotion and grief. I know there is disruption, disquiet, and fracture. But what happens in death? What happens to life? Death brings despair for some while others find hope and affirm resurrection in it.

Have I ever adequately answered that question? The experience of my mum's death has shaped me because it made me address the meaning questions in life. It also made me one who had had to think about death as a part of life in life in a more than cursory way.

At theological college, as both intellectual and emotional resolution of that which remained mystery to me, I wrote a project on death and dying. My mum's death shaped questions that were crucial to my learning and my formation.

The Stations of the Cross project enabled us as community to reflect on these important questions of finitude and mortality and to hold them in conversation with the Christian tradition.

Through this project and these art works I have found a way to hold together the existential questions that I face in pastoral ministry in a way that links who I am as pastoral theologian and as artist and in a way that enables us to engage the wider and dominant culture in accessible ways.

Until the day I die I will still be asking the question of what happens in death. And I will draw on the Christian tradition to help me understand the mystery.

I wonder if the generation of my adult children is putting off having children almost as a direct response to their lack of concern about death? Death doesn't easily or readily break into their lives. There is a certainty about life and health and medicine that keeps the questions at bay. As long as they don't have to answer the hard existential questions that death brings they don't have to think in terms of procreation.

So, maybe the catechetical question is more important than we gave it credit for: What is the purpose of life? What is the purpose—indeed, is there a purpose—in this journey from birth to death? Is there more to life than existing, working, earning, and recreating?

It is these questions that are addressed—or perhaps, better, shaped—in the Stations of the Cross project. In the story that the Stations of the Cross tells there is an important reference to the faith tradition in which I stand and by which I am formed and transformed. There are no absolute answers, only good questions that are answered in the stories that are told over and over to shape and form identity as God's people.

The death of my dad gets into this too. My mum was thirty-five when she died and seemed to disappear from my life. She had gone to the city for treatment (we lived in the country.) I went to stay with relatives for nine months. Somehow I had learned that she was very ill and would likely die. Dad, however, was eighty-two when eventually the day of his death came so many years later. He had been ill for almost ten years, so there were lots of times to sit quietly with him and to reflect, think, and talk about what death would be for him. It was in one of the low times that he looked at me intensely and asked if I knew how to die. As I've said earlier, I said, "You will know how to die when the time comes."

So the importance of the Stations is that they allow people to talk about their own mortality from a slight distance. It is difficult to talk about our own mortality, but possible as discipline of meditative prayer to think on Jesus' journey to death. Thinking or praying the story of Jesus journey of that last painful week enables us to think about our own mortality, even though the recognition that we are reflecting about our own mortality might not be conscious.

The Stations project became important in a different way—a way that I did not expect. It became a most significant part in my rediscovering, renewing, and reclaiming my vocation as a theological teacher. In the days immediately before the exhibition was opened, some colleague ministers asked me, if they brought their parishioners along would I help them to know how to look at the paintings? I offered to lead some guided lecture tours of the works. The people came and found the lecture tours really helpful; in these talks I was reclaiming my vocation as a theological teacher in a context much larger than an academic classroom. The many dimensions of my vocation (academic, pastor, and artist) seemed to come together in a new and rewarding way. Things that I had thought about being a public theologian while in academia seemed in the St. Ives parish to become a practicing reality. In the second year I gave twelve lecture tours talking about the art and artists, and the spiritual journey that flows from engaging our mortality and finitude to more than three hundred and fifty people. The responses of the people suggested that I was breaking open theological ideas and understandings to people I would never have spoken to while I was in the seminary.

At the "Bread and Wine" reception that we set up on Maundy Thursday to share this project with the public, all the work seemed justified when a visitor came up to me and said, "Thank you. I was looking for a deep experience of Easter and I have had it."

A Commentary for the Artists and Viewers of the Stations of the Cross

Growing from my own encounter with and praying of the Stations of the Cross I wrote a pastorally informed commentary that I offered to the artists to guide their initial thinking. I did not want artists just to illustrate the traditional stations with (pious) images of Jesus. I wanted them to engage their own lived experience and to ask and address the existential questions thrown up by their own living. I hoped for images that would engage the viewers in the deep places of their living and open the possibility that the voice of God might break into their lives in fresh ways. I had chosen the artists because they were good artists, not because they were religious or Christian. I wanted them to be free to engage their lived experience in the contemporary world and not to make painting what they thought we might have wanted as a church.

When you engage the Stations you walk sequentially from one to fifteen. In the Franciscan tradition there are generally fourteen stations. We have chosen to follow an adaptation that adds a fifteenth station to represent the resurrection. Somehow, when we walk from one to another of the stations we are enacting the journey of life. The journey (in this case) might not be logical and straightforward.

1 **Jesus Is Condemned to Die**—Each of us learns at some point in our lives of our own mortality that we are going to die. The circumstances and time when we learn that in our deeper being vary greatly.

2 **Jesus Carries His Cross**—Learning of our own mortality is in many senses the cross that we carry through our lives from the moment we become conscious of our mortality.

3 **Jesus Falls the First Time**—We often "stumble" or fall under the weight of the knowledge that we will one day die. The more imminent that death seems, the harder the fall.

4 **Jesus Meets His Mother**—How differently we relate to the person who gave us birth when we realize that she and we are mortal.

5 **Simon Helps Jesus Carry His Cross**—We can't carry the knowledge of our mortality alone. We need others who will help us carry the burden.

6 **Veronica Wipes Jesus' Face**—On the journey, there are often intimate others who help us by attending to our intimate needs.

7 **Jesus Falls the Second Time**—Our mortality continues to be a heavy burden to carry and we fall many times under its weight.

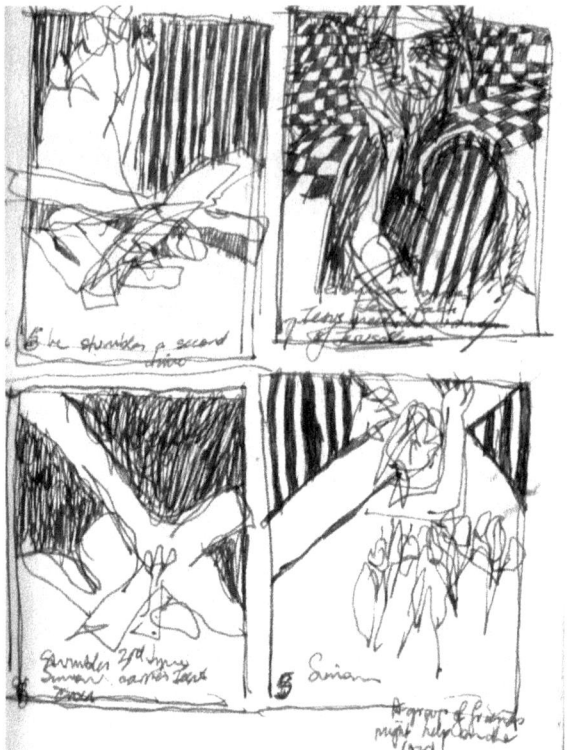

8 **Jesus Meets the Women of Jerusalem**—New Zealand artist Colin McCahon seemed to me to spend his life painting the Stations of the Cross, sometimes consciously and sometimes unconsciously. His large "I AM" paintings seem to me to reflect a knowledge of, and confidence in, his own being. The I AM paintings seem to me to be like Jesus meeting the women of Jerusalem. Something about being in their presence enabled him to say, "I AM."[5]

9 **Jesus Falls the Third Time**—Again, our knowledge of our mortality is a heavy burden and we stumble, fall under its weight, even in those moments when we are able to say "I AM."

10 **Jesus Is Stripped**—I have often read this as "Jesus is stripped bare." As I watched my father and mother-in-law, among many I have known, become fragile and ill in their later years, I was very aware of how our mortality strips us bare, particularly when we are close to death.

5. Many of McCahon's paintings are viewable on the web.

Being a Theological Interpreter   109

11 **Jesus Is Nailed to the Cross**—The process of dying is not easy. There is often a sense of being nailed to the cross.

12 **Jesus Dies on the Cross**—We die, as Jesus died. What is death? What is it when we "are no more"?

13 **Jesus Is Taken Down from the Cross**—I have been taken with the power of the pietà for a very long time. Sometimes in the Christian and Western community we give so much emphasis to the death on the cross that we forget the people at the foot of the cross who hold that battered and beaten and, now dead, Jesus. Can there be any more painful thing in life than for the mother who gave him birth to hold her tortured and murdered son in his death?

14 **Jesus Is Laid in the Tomb**—There is something here of the dignity of the community that lays in their resting places the bodies of the ones who die. They are forced to reflect on all the questions raised by mortality and finitude, and often in the process draw on religious rituals to help find meaning in the death.

15 **Jesus Is Raised to Life**—This station is not typically included as one of the traditional stations. It raises the question of how we find hope in the face of our mortality and finitude.

The Artists' Engagement with Their Own Lived Experience

In the first year of the Stations project, I was continually surprised by the artists' connections with their lived experience. I wanted this connection and I hoped for this connection to occur but I could not have anticipated just how poignant the connections would be.

Garry Foye had drawn station number 2, Jesus takes up his cross. Garry talked about the pain that was in his own body. Because of an injury to his back he experienced great pain and was dependent on daily morphine to survive. He knew in his own life what it was to carry the cross of his mortality.

Jenny Little had drawn Station number 4, Jesus meets his mother. I have known Jenny for a very long time and I knew that her relationship with her own mother was, in her words, "problematic." I knew that this would not have been an easy station for her to paint. It was going to demand honesty and integrity and an emotional openness. She created a work using computerized light that flowed rhythmically and many looked and were moved deeply by their engagement with the created image.

Colina Grant was allocated Station number 5, Simon helps Jesus carry his cross. Colina had been quite ill with cancer in the previous twelve months. She had not painted for some time and was unsure that she could complete the task. Her work is very realistic. She thought on the task for some time, then thought of the many hands that had reached out to help her in the time of her illness: doctors, nurses, family, and friends. So she asked her husband and son to pose with their hands wrapped around each other's wrists. The image she painted had one arm reaching in from the top of the painting and grasping and pulling the other arm that seemed to be drowning in a dark and chaotic world. There was a subtle cross bar that broke the image into the shape of a cross. And she told a story that moved all who heard it. When she was in hospital her young grandson came into the ward. When he saw his grandmother in bed he spontaneously went to the sink, got a face cloth, squeezed the water from it, then came and wiped his grandmother's face.

Euan Macleod had painted a large two-meter-square canvas with a Central Australian landscape and a dark figure walking forward, the head of the figure lost in the shadow of the land. Euan had been asked to paint Station number 10, Jesus is stripped. I visited his studio and he told me about his work. "Often," he said, "my father is the subject of my painting; but that is not so in this case." Then he told me about his dad. He got Alzheimer's at an early age and died when Euan was young. I looked at the image and saw the head lost in the shadow: "Isn't that what you have painted?" I asked, "Isn't that what Alzheimer's is? The body is there, but the head (brain, mind) has gone missing?" "Well, it is a painting of my dad then," he said. During the exhibition I introduced a group of people with early stages of Alzheimer's to the works. When I told them this story, one of the women, a medical doctor, said loudly "I can identify with that."

I did not manage to have a conversation with Russel Carey about his work before the exhibition. We managed a couple of brief phone conversations. He had been asked to paint Station 12, Jesus dies on the Cross. A couple of times he said to me, "I'm an atheist, you know." I assured him that didn't matter to me. When Russell brought his painting of Jesus crucified on a telegraph pole in the inner city it had a poignant beauty. I thought to myself you could not paint an image as lovingly as you have painted this image without some deep feeling for the pain of death and dying. And the light rose from the base of the painting. The image of one dying was filled with hope. My guess: Russell knows what it is to find light in darkness.

And Chris Wyatt, whose work I wrote about earlier. Chris was allocated Station 14, Jesus is laid in the tomb. Knowing that Chris had laid the body of his wife Catriona in the tomb just nine months before, I wanted to save him from this painting. But I could not do that. As he painted the work I knew that in some way Chris would be continuing the long slow process of burying Catriona. His image had a large group of people carrying Jesus toward the grave. Jesus was inverted. His head was lower than his feet and his arm stretched out making for an upside down cross shape. When you looked closely at the painting you can see that Jesus was being lowered into a chasm or void. In the top two thirds of the painting all the figures were living, in the bottom one third there were skeletons and skulls and a snake and darkness. Chris knew (and I knew that he knew because we had talked about it together) that he would have to enter a void, a place of darkness before he could experience the light of a new day. His image of that moment of awful darkness that comes with the loss of a loved one in death was filled in the warmest way with hope and possibility.

These artists (and the others whose work I have not named,) all seemed to touch the lived experience that encounters darkness and had found light within that darkness. Their works speak of resurrection and promise hope.

6

Being and Doing in Ministry: Being

LONELINESS

I'M SITTING ALONE IN an Asian food shop eating a hot chicken laksa for lunch. I have just come from being with a couple in an intensive care unit. She had had some serious preventative surgery for what had been a life-threatening malfunction in her body. He put his arm around me and leant his head on my shoulder as I prayed for them.

I'm consumed this morning with the loneliness of parish ministry. I get sick of eating my lunch alone in my office or, today, in the Asian food shop.

That feeling of aloneness is odd given that when I am visiting people in their homes they tell me how lucky they are to have me as minister and that I talk with them as though I have been a long-time friend.

So there I was, sitting alone, eating my lunch, and writing on my small computer, when a parishioner happened to come by and greeted me. The reason I sit in the public space is to be open to these chance encounters. It was an important one: she apologized for walking past me on the way out of church and not stopping to speak. "I had been crying and my face was all puffy and I didn't want to talk," she said. I asked if something had happened in church to cause her tears. "No. Other stuff just leaking out. Don't know why it happened in church." She didn't seem to want to talk further about it. I told her I thought it appropriate that we touch the deep things in church; that is what it is about. "I often used to leave church via the side door when I was a parishioner, because when I touched the deep places I needed the space to be alone," I tell her.

How different being alone is from being lonely. When I want to be alone (and I need to be alone about 50 percent of the time), I want space to be with my self and my own thoughts. I am alone when I go into my studio and paint, I am alone when I write, I am alone when I am walking and cycling, I am alone when I go aside to pray, I am alone when I read and when I listen to music. Loneliness is different.

I am lonely when nobody calls, when nobody wants me because I'm me. I feel lonely when no one says to me, "Come for a coffee" (and implied, a time of conversation, of connecting, of being). I am lonely when I think or assume or imagine that no one is interested in the life of my soul.

I was eating the very best laksa. The person who had stopped to be with me asked with care whether I was enjoying being the minister in this parish. She pondered ministering to an older group of people, suggesting that I must deal a lot with illness and death—which of course I do. "It must be draining," she suggested. "Whom do you talk to?" I told her that I found it "energizing when people talked openly about their lives. And I'm going to Melbourne for an annual retreat with a group of colleagues. We eat, drink, yell, and play together. We each give an account of our lives and ministry, and we worship. I find that really helpful. We've been going away like this for thirty years. And I will go to Melbourne a little early so I can have a longer conversation with a colleague who is a friend to my soul."

I wrote to a friend overseas saying how I struggled with this loneliness, and he wrote back saying things that seemed to touch and nurture my soul. I felt known.

The church at the moment seems into "management speak," and ministers are told they should not have friends in their parish. "It is not appropriate," they are told, "for ministers to marry from within the parish, and if they choose to become engaged to be married to someone in the parish, the fiancé should worship somewhere else, because this would be an inappropriate pastoral relationship." And, they say, you cannot be friends with your parishioners. All this intrigues me. It sets up a paradigm for lonely ministers. After all, who ministers to the pastor's family then? How does the church support lonely ministers? The expressed taboo on building friendships in the parish (with like-minded people, who hold similar values) seems to push people like me who need such friendships into places of accentuated loneliness and makes them very vulnerable.

I have always worked well in teams and with communities of people. I find it difficult to work alone.

Some would push me towards a professional relationship with a counselor, or a supervisor, or a spiritual director. "Go and talk to them about your loneliness," they say. I'm not sure that paying someone to listen to me resolves the deeper issue.

There is more to this question of loneliness: it is about friendship, about intimacy, about being wanted, about being touched physically and emotionally, about being recognized, about being important, about being successful, about living authentically. It is about being able to recognize and have affirmed what my life calls out in me.

It is resolved by being in good friendships, caring communities, and working at my intimate relationships, especially the one with Heather, my wife.

Why do I go around with this heavy sensation of loneliness in my heart? Why do I long for someone to call me on the phone, to want to spend time with me, to want me?

And suddenly the commitment to visit people in the parish makes me forget my own hunger to be wanted.

Later, I ring a colleague and ask whether he has time for coffee. We sit in the sunshine and talk. I ask him whether he is ever lonely in ministry. "Yes. Sometimes the people in the congregation just don't get it. They are affirming in words, say they are supportive, but don't—and perhaps can't—understand the grey areas of ministry." We begin to talk about what makes the role of the ordained person unique and what it is to live and work as the "ordained person" in a community.

The loneliness was eased. I was talking with a person who knew.

NO, NOT AVAILABLE

In the middle of the night I woke thinking about a conversation that I'd had earlier in the day. Over coffee my voice had become a sort of refrain as this friend told me what was happening in his life. I kept saying to him: "No. Not available!" I was trying to encourage him to set some limits on his availability. Now, at 3 a.m., I had to ask myself why wasn't I able to live the "No. Not available" message myself? I should be sleeping.

I've always thought I was good at setting clear limits to my availability. I have valued time with my wife and family as a space for meeting my needs for intimacy, and know that without meeting those needs I cannot be appropriately present to others.

But recently, you'll recall, I'd chosen to take two days out of my holiday to come back to the city and conduct a funeral for Faye. Previously I'd been in team ministries and could rely on others to conduct funerals when I was away. So conducting this funeral was a compromise I wanted to make because I had "walked with" Faye and Roger and the family and thought that "walking with them" should involve the funeral as well. It was a choice that I was happy to make and that I had negotiated with Heather, my wife.

Setting clear boundaries and limits is hard work. I recall working with a young woman in a hospital setting. She was struggling to become an independent adult person. I encouraged her, saying that perhaps she should move out from her parents' home. She quickly put me in my place: "I have done that a number of times, and every time I move out, my mum goes into hospital, and I've got to come back home to look after her and Dad." I felt powerless at the difficulty of her journey. Another time, just as I was getting my kids into the car to leave on holiday after worship services, someone who had been at church rang to say she was going to kill herself. I listened, and then encouraged her to talk with someone else, yelled inappropriately at my kids, and left for vacation. Another time Elsie, who was in her nineties, was close to death. I went to the hospital on Friday afternoon, told her I was running a weekend retreat for the church, that I would return to see her on Sunday evening. I returned to the hospital Sunday evening, as I had promised, fed Elsie her evening meal, and went home. She died peacefully not long after I left the hospital.

How do I say, "No. Not available" when relationships become dysfunctional and I am being hooked in and think that only I can solve this problem? I am made important when people need me to help and I think I am the only one who can help.

When someone asked Pablo Picasso what was his greatest gift as an artist, he replied, "My strong sense of my own self." That sense of self is crucial to being able to say: "No. Not available."

There is another important part of being able to say "No. Not available," and that is knowing how I meet my needs for intimacy, and working to nourish those intimate times and spaces. I reflected with my friend on times when I had been away from home working, when the offer of a sexual relationship was strongly hinted at, if not explicitly made. In those times I've typically rather clumsily said, "I'm married and enjoy the sexual relationship that I have with my wife." Even now, years later, I'm struggling to find the right combination of words to express that. Saying "No. Not available" in these settings takes both a strong sense of self and finding ongoing ways and places to appropriately meet my needs for intimacy.

When I wake in the middle of the night thinking on these things I know that it is going to be a lifelong struggle.

So what does that look like, practically?

In my marriage, we create spaces for our own intimacy, for example by regularly going out for dinner or to a movie by ourselves. This way we have time to build a functioning intimate relationship. Heather knows how important it is that we do that; ours is a mutual commitment to shared intimacy. One perhaps unusual way we maintain such intimacy is as a result of living in our own home some distance from the parish that I serve, and therefore still close to our old church where Heather continues to worship. This means my lover is not part of the congregation where I minister, and Heather doesn't have her lover as the "God person" leading worship for her. It is possible that we are better lovers because of that.

BORING

Reflection is hard work. Sometimes I can sit down and write because the issue is accessible, and sometimes, like today, I want to put it off.

An elder in the congregation had asked me to visit a family on the fringe of the church. I did not know that he had been ill and recently hospitalized. The illness had confined him to his home and the dreamed-of trips in his retirement years had been put on hold.

I went to visit, knowing little about the family or why I would be visiting. I had called and asked if it would be appropriate for me to visit, and as I walked up the front steps I was thinking: I will just ask about their lives. I will just try to get to know them. I didn't have any memory of meeting them at church. I didn't have any conscious knowledge of his recent illness.

I went in and found that he was propped up in a large lounge chair in front of the TV. Movement looked difficult.

I asked about the illness, about retirement, about the work he and she had done before retirement, about their plans for travel, about their family, about the sport they had played past and present, about where they had lived and traveled, about the work their children do, about their family relationships, and about their grandchildren. All my questions were trying to find points of connection. You came from that area, my daughter taught in that area; you lived in that city, I lived in that city; you have grandchildren, I have a grandchild; you support that football team, I support that football team. "What do you think of their chances of winning this week?" There was little response to anything.

I stayed for more than an hour, then took my leave. I didn't feel it appropriate to offer to pray with them; that would have been too intimate. Then again, maybe it would have taken the conversation to a deeper place and established why I was there. What stopped me from holding their lives on open palms before God and asking for both healing and blessing?

As I drove away, quite honestly I was thinking, "How boring was that?" For all my trying I didn't think that we had made any connection at all. How hard pastoral ministry is when I find the people boring, when I can't get beyond the surface to make a connection with their lived experience. How hard pastoral ministry is when I don't feel that I'm fulfilling any useful purpose. In the back of my head are these rational thoughts: I do think that any contact with people is important, that being in people's homes is important; that when I come as priestly person that I am a symbolic presence of God's care and grace, and I do think that when I visit I am getting to know people so that when there is a crisis I can enter the conversation more easily. But this particular visit, this particular day, I was simply bored.

When I told a good colleague about my boredom, she said, "It has to do with them, not you." "Not so," I said, "the boredom is in me. I have to look at what is happening in me. What did I contribute to having such a boring conversation?" When my children were younger and complained of being bored I would say to them, "Boredom is alright. It doesn't hurt to be bored. If you stay with being bored for a while you will discover something else to do." I might have learned that from something I think Picasso said: boredom is the basis of creativity.

Yet just at the moment I can't quite see how this boring conversation might be the basis of something creative. Time might reveal the way.

GETTING LOST

Being lonely, setting limits, being bored, and this story of getting lost are all ultimately about what is going on inside me. It is easy to blame the other person, to keep it "out there." All the things that happen to me in my living become the stuff of my daily reflection. If—as in this piece—I pretend that being lost has nothing to do with me, if I see it as a matter of bad maps or being in a rush, I learn little. Each incident like this shapes how I learn to function better in ministry. It is about accepting responsibility for the life that I live.

I got incredibly and inexplicably lost driving between the home of one parishioner and of the home of another parishioner one Sunday afternoon. It had been a quiet week for me. Someone else had preached in the morning service and the early spring sunshine seemed to give me energy to visit a couple of families it is difficult to visit mid-week because the members work. The drive should have taken five minutes but I made a wrong turn, then tried to take short cuts that are impossible in Sydney because no road goes in a straight line and creeks, rivers, and ravines riddle the cityscape. The house I was to visit was on the very edge of the map I was trying to read and I really needed the adjacent maps too. I became flustered because I was late and tried to guess where I needed to go. I misread a street sign and drove past where I was meant to be. Then I found myself on a major road going in the wrong direction yet again. I turned into a side street, acknowledged that I was very lost, took some deep breaths, and read the map again and more closely. I was now half an hour beyond the time I had said I would visit. That was not as important as the fact that I had taken more than half an hour to drive a distance that should have taken me five minutes at most. What was going on? Why was I allowing myself to become so flustered and so distressed that I could not read the street directory? That was not like me. I usually read maps well and navigate my way confidently.

I apologized for my late arrival and enjoyed being present in another's home, which, as someone once told me, is like being invited into the person.

Later, driving home, I began to wonder what had happened to me that I became so lost. Perhaps it was that earlier in the day I had listened to a story that disturbed me. It wasn't difficult for the person who told me, for he had long since come to terms with it, but it left me sad and powerless and uncertain. For I had no capacity to change what had happened; you can't undo the past. I had gone to these people's home to hear the story of their lived experience and to value that story, as a way of honoring their souls. They told me the story with integrity; I acknowledged their lives and asked God's blessing upon them. But the story broke into my being and I lost my way. Perhaps I just needed time and space to process what I had heard before I could move on to be present with others. And perhaps there was something here for my soul, something in the story of my life that needed attention.

BROKEN GLASS

One early spring afternoon, I was riding my bike, saying a Jesus mantra, and getting into the rhythm of pedaling, when suddenly I found myself trying to pick my way through a whole lot of broken glass. Someone had smashed a bottle on the path and I knew that one little shard of glass could puncture my tire. As I stood up on the pedals and peered carefully down at the bike path looking for a way through, a dream image flashed into mind. In the dream I was in a room trying to get through and the floor was covered in broken glass. I couldn't get through without standing on the glass. The choice I had was whether to stand on the large or the small pieces, and I was scared about what damage would be done to my feet.

It was a bit disturbing. What had I done to shape a dream like that? As quickly as the dream had come to me, I remembered the meeting the previous evening when I had shared with the elders some suggestions for things we could do in ministry. I wouldn't have wanted to admit to myself or to anyone else that there was a sense of walking on broken glass as I presented my suggestions, but that is what I heard my dream saying.

I had spent eight months being present to the people, listening to them and listening to the community, and I had written a number of suggestions as to possibilities for ministry and now I was sharing them. I was reminded of long ago having heard an art therapist say that when an artist puts a painting on the wall, it is in a way their "self," so when people talk about whether or not they like the painting, they are in effect talking about the person who painted it. Presenting these ideas to the elders had a similar feeling of self-exposure and vulnerability to it. It was as though I were walking on broken glass.

There are times when we make the people in the church powerless by saying to them, "Suggest what we should do in ministry and mission" and the people don't really know and so they suggest the things that have always been done, and then we "beat them up" for having no imagination. I think as the spiritual leader of the community it is my responsibility to listen and then with imagination make achievable suggestions as to what the community might do. I made my suggestions with the clearly stated (written) understanding that these might be very good ideas and it would be appropriate for us to say, "these are good ideas, important suggestions but we don't have the personal resources, energy, or finance to do them and so we can say 'no' without having to feel guilty."

I'm also scared about what responsibility I will have to take in seeing the suggestions that I made come to life. Yes, I was walking on broken glass and it is important that I acknowledge how much presenting these ideas demanded of me.

PICKING MY HEAD

I'd been picking at my head for months. Eventually my wife persuaded me to go to the doctor. I went because I was sick of this constant picking. I thought I had a bad case of dandruff. "Not so," said the doctor, "you have psoriasis." With some optimism he told me he could alleviate it, but that I'd always have it and that it would be worse in winters than in summers. At my initial visit the doctor told me that psoriasis was inherited and was usually brought on by stress. Have you been under any stress lately?, he asked. Well yes, and I documented for him some of my employment history in the preceding eighteen months. Without the slightest hint of a smile, he told me that people like me had to learn to forgive.

Quite honestly, I saw that "you-people-have-to-learn-to-forgive" comment as a bit of a joke. I'd been an academic pastoral theologian for ten years. I had read some of the best books on forgiveness. Why, only in June, I had met Jim Emerson in the United States and told him that his book on forgiveness[1] had shaped my life. The need to provide an environment in which forgiveness might be experienced has been so important to me throughout my ministry. And here was a doctor telling me that I needed to learn about forgiveness.

Perhaps, just perhaps, he was right.

But the psoriasis hasn't gone away. I still find myself in private moments and, sometimes in public, picking at my head. My wife now asks, "What is stressing you?" when she sees me picking at my head. "Well, I have an exhibition in three weeks that is going to cost me three thousand dollars, and I have to hope that I will sell enough paintings to cover the costs. And the publishers have said 'no' to my book and I have to find somewhere else to get it published. And I'm trying to think into a sermon for Sunday. How will I lead appropriate worship that nourishes the lives of the people? And I've outlined some dreams for what the congregation will do and I

---

1. Emerson, *Dynamics of Forgiveness*.

see the process of implementing these things as being really demanding. And I'm going to a doctoral seminar with a student I am supervising. And I'm trying to find someone to lead worship in a month's time so that we can go away on holidays."

When I name all those things I realize that perhaps there are more things stressing me than I have been willing to acknowledge. I know that I need friends with whom I can verbalize these stressful things, so I call someone and talk, and also write in my journal. While writing in my journal a phrase emerges that disturbs and stresses me too. I find myself writing that "I feel like an outsider to life." That's another indicator of the stress that I'm feeling. I do things to try to balance my life: I exercise regularly, paint, draw, go out for dinner with my wife, cook good food, enjoy good wine, connect with significant others. Yet at times I still feel the loneliness that finds its expression in these frightening words, "sometimes I feel like an outsider to life."

At this point in the writing I find my left arm reaching up (unconsciously) to pick at my head. Stupid, really.

About twelve months later I finally resolved that I wanted to be rid of the bitterness that had accrued in my soul. With the doctor's words about learning to forgive still ringing in my head I decided to preach a sermon on the line in the Lord's Prayer, "as we forgive those who sin against us."

As I prepared to preach on this passage a number of difficult things were going on around me, including that I was learning about the breakdown of my son and daughter-in-law's marriage, a loved parishioner was dying, and I was continuing to struggle emotionally with the lack of acknowledgement of my contribution in the theological college. During the week of preparing for worship I wondered on the words "As we forgive those who sin against us": is there a harder call in Christian faith? How easy, I thought, to go with the sense that if we make confession of the wrongs we have done, God forgives what we have done and all is well. I wondered how it would change if we were a little more open in saying "God forgives to the degree, to the measure, that we make space for the sinned against to forgive us."

I read the *Wounded Heart of God*,[2] in which Andrew Sung Park describes how the doctrinal focus of the church has been on the forgiveness of the offenders, not the forgivingness of the victims. The church has emphasized the forgiveness of our sin. Park opened my eyes to the importance of the forgivingness of the victims. He pointed out that the doctrines of justification and salvation have forgotten the wronged. It slowly began to dawn on me that the model used in worship where the priestly person pronounces forgiveness on behalf of God has been to our cost both as individuals and as nations. Jesus focused on the victims and his philosophy of forgiveness grew from the perspective of the oppressed. In the sermon I wanted to say that the emphasis of the church has been on the forgiveness of the wrongdoer, but in Jesus' teaching in the Lord's Prayer the emphasis is on the forgivingness of the wronged: "forgive us our sins, *as we forgive those who sin against us.*"

It was a really important milestone in my journey. How do I forgive those who I think were advantaged by my disadvantage? How do I forgive those who I think shamed me? We want oppressed peoples to find freedom—whether they be the indigenous peoples of our countries, political prisoners, victims of wars international and civil, or of broken relationships. I thought of the difficulty when the perpetrator has been advantaged by the disadvantage of the other. But, rather than thinking of remote possibilities, my question had to have a significant connection with my life: How do I forgive when I have been the one disadvantaged? It is the most difficult thing that my faith asks of me. Then there was another question: How could I preach on this so that it is not just an indulgence? One part of me wanted dramatically to take off my alb when I began the sermon, and say to the people, "I am not so much bringing the Word of God today as asking for help to live the Word of God." How many thousands of times I have prayed those words and how futile is my living of them? ". . . as we forgive those who sin against us."

The sermon touched people deeply. It wasn't just me who struggled to live out forgivingness.

I also realized that the structure of our liturgy in which a "priestly person" says to the people "Your sins are forgiven," works in favor of the sinner rather than the sinned against. I rewrote the liturgy to say: God, give us the grace to forgive those who have hurt us.

---

2. Sung Park, *Wounded Heart*.

Enable us to provide a space for those whom we have offended to forgive us.

May we be a forgiven and forgiving people.
By the grace of God, Amen.

With all the usual anxiety I led worship on Sunday, and after it was over, a woman who was still a stranger to me came up to me, took my hand, and said, "Every week you nourish my soul." I could not have a more significant piece of feedback than that. That is what I want to do. That is my role, to nourish the souls of the people. When I get feedback like that it significantly reduces the stress for somehow I am energized by what is happening for this one person.

The psoriasis will always be there. I hope that it doesn't have to dominate my life.

After preaching this sermon, I was somehow set free, and in the ensuing days I threw out sixteen years of teaching notes. I told a couple of colleagues about doing this. Their response was a stunned silence; and I knew that the silence reflected a grief in them for what had happened and the realization that I was letting that part of my life go.

KNOCKED FLAT

It is Sunday evening. I have been absolutely wiped out by the sermon I preached this morning. I came home and fell asleep in front of the TV and some hours later I still feel spent. I've learned that some things in ministry take a lot more energy than the time involved. The funeral service for an out-of-place death can take energy way in excess of the time it takes to conduct the funeral. In such an instance, there is a funny mix of the adrenalin rush that accompanies being invited into the intimate space of people in deep grief and being the "important person" who leads the funeral, and the emotional energy needed to minister appropriately to the needs of the many people who gather.

My sermon this morning was about a series of questions I would put to Jesus after I had read the question the Pharisees put to Jesus in Mark 10. They asked a "trick" question about whether the law would allow a man to divorce his wife. I told the people that I would want to ask Jesus about how we are "bodies," gendered bodies. What might he say about gender when it is unclear? What would Jesus say to us about being created male and female, and sexuality and procreation and the birth rate in the present age and how we meet our sexual needs, and emotional and sexual intimacy? I'd ask Jesus how he understood marriage and I'd ask about his understanding of marriage as an economic unit. And then I'd want to acknowledge the importance of his comment about a man leaving his father and mother and joining with his wife and the two becoming one flesh. But I'd want to know what Jesus thought about the two becoming one when they didn't become one or when the oneness became unstuck. In other words I'd want to know what he thought about the breakdown of marriage and divorce.

I spoke as one who has lived in a long-term marriage that has enabled me to live the fullness of my being. I outlined a number of things that might contribute to successful marriage (stability of family of origin, an awareness of identity, shared life values and goals, an ability to communicate in words and body, a mutual commitment to seek the best for the other, a commitment to work at the marriage, and a willingness to do things that nourish the marriage. Happy children do not necessarily make a happy marriage but a happy marriage does make for happy children.)

Then I talked about the mystery of when the "two become one" doesn't work. I talked about my brother this week asking me to conduct his third marriage and how I saw marriage as created for joy and not pain, and that I would bless his marriage because I think when we do that we are providing the space for people to experience forgiveness and to get on with their lives.

Marriage remains a mystery. Sometimes it works in ways that bless the people and other times it hurts people. From outside I can't understand what goes on in other people's marriages.

This church has run divorce recovery groups for nearly twenty years. One of the things that I like about the congregation is that it provides a community in which people who have experienced divorce can belong. I wanted to affirm their belonging on a day when the biblical text we read in church could be interpreted as being quite judgmental of people who have been divorced and remarried.

Finally I told a story about patience in marriage. When I had been teaching a course on marriage, I divided marriage up into about fifteen different phases from cohabiting, becoming engaged, married with small children, to married fifty years, widowed, and so on. Students had to interview people about their experience of marriage at particular stages and bring a report of that interview to share with the class. One day a young, single, Korean student brought the report of his conversation with a couple who had been married sixty years. It was a fascinating story of an arranged marriage when the two were eighteen. It included a long separation while he worked in Vietnam and then their migration to Australia. The "westernized" student asked if they had ever said to each other "I love you?" I cringed as I listened. They hadn't and he asked, "Would you like to do that now?" and they did it. Then he asked what they thought was the most important thing in marriage, and the husband said, "Patience." What a wise statement. Then I realized that is one of the ways Paul described love in 1 Corinthians 13, but I had never heard it like that before. So I told the people about the importance of patience in long marriages.

I wanted to affirm people in their marriages, I wanted to touch people who were married and had been widowed, I wanted to say to people who have been divorced and remarried that they have a place here where they belong, and I wanted to help all the people present to value patience as a part of their love.

A number of people came to thank me after the service. The one that stands out is a woman who said: "It is my birthday and I am going home to celebrate with my husband of forty-three years and my gay daughter." I had not been aware that her daughter was gay until she told me this day. Four couples who had partners who had previously been divorced came to touch me, and thank me. Others came to celebrate their (long) marriages with me. Some came with their "uncomfortable jokes," such as "I'm patient in my marriage; I always say, 'yes.'"

Giving reflections in church, standing in front of the people without the security of being in the pulpit and without notes is always emotionally demanding and I feel vulnerable. I have learned to accept that when I forget things that I had thought were important during the preparation that they probably weren't that important. I had thought hard about the difference between protecting the cultural institutions of marriage and family, and relationships that are just and fair. I omitted to say that, and on reflection later realized that these things were implicit in what I had spoken. They didn't need to be explicit.

After the service I take a space a bit to the side of the main exit. People can bypass me if they want to. Yet many people seek me out, wanting to acknowledge what had happened for them in the service and the sermon; they want to let me know. And I sought to attend to them all. Being present in intense moments with a lot of different people one on top of the other is demanding.

And then I came home exhausted, physically and emotionally. It is not always like this. I was talking into their lived experience in intimate relationship. I knew that while there had been controversies in the wider church about these things, these people would listen openly and be grateful for words spoken that were relevant to their daily living. At the same time there is always the uncertainty that I might upset people. I had begun the sermon saying, "These things are emotional and if what I say today disturbs you, please come and talk with me about it."

When I got home I had lunch and fell asleep. When I woke I had that weird sense of being unable to move physically, as though I were still asleep. Nobody who had been present at worship would have any inkling, I think, that what took me an hour in the day, and perhaps twenty minutes of that hour, could have taken so much energy and could have left me so tired.

NOURISHMENT: RETREAT

It's Saturday morning and I'm staying at my friend's home in Melbourne on the way to our annual retreat, which I described earlier in the book, thinking myself into the days to come. This was the following year.

It is an informal retreat with no institutional backing. I would go a long way to be part of this retreat. Nairn had died not long after the last retreat, Alex or "Ferg" had died twenty years earlier. The really interesting thing to me is that those who have participated in this retreat have all stayed in ministry.

The retreat this year was different for me. I was in a very different place.

Nine of us had gathered at Lorne. Sadly, Keith was ill, and couldn't make it.

We ate a lot, drank considerably less than we used to, even though there was some very good whisky and a lot of quality red wines. Stories of previous times together were told and retold. Nairn and Alex, who have died, were named, recalled in affectionate story, and toasted.

Robert introduced us to the text for next Sunday, and—no planning, it just happened—he raised a good question: What nourishes or sustains you? I thought: "Being with you guys. Doing this is what gets me through long term."

After talking over the text, each of us in turn took an hour to give an account of our life and ministry over the past twelve months.

There was some disciplined listening and tough responding. This was a place where we were accountable for our lives. I told of my journey back to parish ministry, and also of the pain that remains in me for how I have been treated by the church. My friends could see that I was still hurting and angry; at the same time they recognized, named, and affirmed the distance they had seen me come in the last year. As each person spoke, I drew him or her. It is a good way for me to both practice my drawing and to listen. I seem to get better each year at getting their likenesses—though at one stage John looked over my shoulder, and with his deep hearty laugh, told me that I had drawn a number of people twenty years younger than they were.

I always need some space alone, and I seem to need literally to play with paint every day, so I had taken some paper and paint and disappeared for a few minutes whenever I could to put another layer of paint on some paintings. I wanted to build up a few works on paper over the days we had together.

Alan is another member of the group and he does something similar as a photographer. He takes some time away from the group to stalk his images with a camera. He doesn't just hold the camera and click. He is much more deliberate, walking, looking, thinking, planning, and finally, photographing. He will keep just a couple of the twenty or so images of the seaside pools, rocks, and waves. Shaping the images is a discipline honed by years of practice and dissatisfaction with the cliché. I learn from him about waiting for the image to come to me.

We shared a big lunch, steak and sausages and salad, sitting around the garden table near the barbeque. Just wonderful to be with people among whom I have the confidence to name all that is in me.

Then, a little later, inside and warmed by the large log fire, we broke bread and drank wine. Peter led us, affirming each of us by name, then recognizing and naming our particular gifts. For all my desire to hear such affirmation, it is difficult for me to hear it when it is given. I have to force myself to listen and acknowledge the words, "your gifts as pastor and in expressing things so clearly both visually and in words. You have so many gifts . . ." "Yes, and I want to live them responsibly."

Peter brought the bread and wine to each of us in turn, naming us, blessing us, and asking us to take the bread and the wine as symbols to remind us that God is with us in all of our living. Big wholesome hugs shared among a special group of friends. The peace of God offered as we did so. Malcolm asked us to be aware of how the bread and wine will link us to all those in the church to come, whose names and lives we cannot yet see. That was a profound thought for me to reflect on.

A few of us walked the five and half kilometers into Lorne along the water's edge, refreshed by the smell of salt, the sound of surf, the mixed aromas of sea and surrounding eucalypt, and getting oxygen into our lungs.

I played my first game of bridge. Some of these guys have played the game every time we have met. Other years I've always been a distant spectator. I'm not yet a convert. I'd rather draw and paint, or sleep the hours they play, and it was good to share the fun of the game.

Going home I felt good. The time with these colleagues had once again been nourishing for my soul. We had enacted an answer to the question Robert had asked of us: "What nourishes and sustains you?"

PRAYER

Many Christians seem uncertain about their private practice when prayer is mentioned. I am no different. The retreat that I have just described is a most important place of prayer for me. Others might imagine when the minister is at prayer it is far more pious and structured.

Iris

I had taken the day as a "prayer day." My life had been intense and I needed to recoup some energy. I drove with friends to the ferry stop, to show them the way, and then I walked the hour and forty minutes home—what I called "prayer time." In order to be a priestly person I need time to pray, to hold the congregation and the tasks of ministry in my heart before God.

That sounds pious. In reality, I walked and thought.

When I arrived home and settled in a chair at my desk the phone rang.

"My name is. . . . I represent 'xyz' charity. How are you today?" The words were out of my mouth before I had time to think. "I choose where I will give my money and don't need to be solicited, thank you." There was a silence and I hung up the phone. I could have (legitimately) said, "My mother's sister has just died and . . ."

A little while later the phone rang again. This time it was Iris. She had been recently widowed. (Iris had been married to Ian, whom I visited in intensive care when he was dying.) She had some confusion about whether I was the person she needed to talk with, confusion about a church roster.

And then confusion about how she felt about her husband's death. "I was ill, I had a stroke and other things, and he looked after me. I was delirious, (and close to death) for four days. Then I got a bit better and he became ill. It was like I got better to look after him and he died, and perhaps I should have died."

I talked about how bewildering and confusing life is sometimes.

Iris made a jump then to tell me that she had been with her daughter-in-law to see the exhibition of my paintings. "There is a lot of anger there." And she began to interpret it, not as anger in me, but anger for the way the world is going, anger for the sort of world we are creating and handing on. She saw crossed marks in the paintings and saw those as representing some of the conflicts in our world. And she saw the intensified color behind the black and could see and name the hope.

I was very affirmed by her response to the work. She read the works as I would want them read. She was letting the works come to her gently, not trying to see something in them, simply and openly responding to the color and line and brush-marks. Her reading was taking her into the space of deep prayer, a serious reflection on life and the world; she was naming herself before God.

I told her how pleased I was to hear her response and how, for me, that is the space of prayer.

My Practice of Prayer

In my role as priestly person, as pastor, almost every time I visit people I offer to pray with them. And every time I offer the people accept. I usually shape a brief prayer that names the people and, as I like to say, holds them on open palms before God. I ask God to bless individuals, marriages, families, relationships, spaces.

Then I go back to the church office and the office secretary asks me for prayer points to put in the church bulletin for Sunday, and I become reluctant and say, "I'm not really a person of prayer." What I mean by that is that pious prayer scares me. We say grace at home before the evening meal, but I'm uncomfortable when people want to say grace in a restaurant. In my head I think that God knows we are grateful and I wonder if the words make any difference. I hope that I live as one whose heart is always open in prayer, but saying that makes me uncomfortable, for it is the way I would want to live, rather than a place at which I have arrived.

And in someone's home, beside a hospital bed, I feel as a pastoral and spiritual leader that I should offer "words." I leave feeling confused: how come I can offer the words in someone else's home and they seem inappropriate in mine?

I'm cynical when people ask if ours is a "praying church," meaning "do they have a prayer meeting?" when the whole community gathers before God in prayer each week. I trust this form of prayer to be adequate.

What is it to pray? I have a number of disciplines that are not "wordy" prayer, and yet I think all are prayer, and together, they shape me. Writing a daily journal, riding a bike, walking, praying a mantra, filling a sketchbook, painting in my studio, thinking reflectively on the Bible passages for the coming Sunday, reading the daily newspaper, lying in bed breathing deeply and slowly and gently drifting in to sleep.

I've been away to monasteries in times past for silent retreats. On one I spent eight days making drawings and walking and meditating and reflecting on the journey with a spiritual director. The discipline of going away on an intentional and focused retreat like this enables me to live with the "openness to God" that I described previously.

I'm not good at intercessory prayer that wants God to change particular things in the world. I can pray for the health and wholeness of my family, but how can I expect God to be more interested in my family than a much less well-off family in Rwanda or Chile or Tonga whose members are starving or political prisoners or victims of civil war?

Preparing for worship each week is part of my prayer discipline. Each Tuesday morning I read the lectionary readings for the coming Sunday. Then I spend the week wondering about the truth that is present in these texts and how I might make that accessible, relevant, and appropriate for the people who will gather to worship. I become aware of the lives of the people I have visited in their homes and in the hospitals and with whom I have talked at the church garage sale. I wonder how these passages will relate to their lived experience and what questions their experience might bring to the texts. That discipline becomes the focus of my thought when I am driving the car, when I am exercising, when I am lying in bed at night. I churn it over and over and over. I sit with a big board on my lap while watching TV and I scribble notes, ideas, and questions. I read commentaries and other texts that come to mind. It is a practice that shapes who I am, and a discipline that I regret I lost while teaching in the seminary. It is a core part of my prayer life.

7

Identity: Memory

A FAMILY FUNERAL: A PLACE TO BE RECONNECTED

When you sit in the back row of a funeral the tears come, perhaps more than when you are in the front row. Deaths in families do strange things. After the death of my mum, and my dad's remarriage, my mum's sisters seemed (to me) to take a backward step and never made contact with us, their sister's children. My cousin had rung me four or five weeks ago to say that his mum—my aunt, and my birth mother's sister—was dying. In that phone conversation he dated our last meeting as 1956 . . . more than fifty years ago. This week he left a message on our answering machine telling me of his mother's death, inviting me to the funeral and to the reception afterwards, where I might meet some of my family who I had not seen in all those years.

After getting Max's message I did something very rare for me: I got up out of bed during the night to write a page in my journal about being "welcome." The words Max left were so warm that I had a sense of belonging: "I belong," I began to say inside my head. "I belong."

I accepted the warm invitation and I drove across to Woronora for my aunt's funeral. As I got near the crematorium I began to wonder. I was uncertain. It crossed my mind that I could drive away: what if I wasn't welcome? I walked a wide circle to find the toilet. Then I came back and saw Ed, my mother's brother and Bet, his wife, (my uncle and aunt). I had lived with them for nine months while my mum was ill. We have kept contact through the years. I walked up to greet them and was soon introduced to others: Gary (my cousin) and Louise, his wife, and Keith, Beryl's younger son, whom I hadn't seen since our grandma's funeral in 1979 and for another twenty-five years before that.

We were ushered in to the service and found a very carefully prepared, presented, and printed order of service. Before I arrived, I had thought I would sit or stand in the back row and have a few quiet tears as I remembered that Beryl was my mum's sister. The service began with four grandchildren reading stories their grandmother had told, and the stories included things that she had done with her sister Elsie. For the first time in my life someone else had a story that included my mum. As I started to sing the first hymn, the tears began to run uncontrollably down my face. I knew what was happening, and why, so I let the tears be there. Then in his eulogy Max named his mum not only as the sister of Ed and Barbara, but also of "Elsie, who sadly died more than fifty years ago." I cried some more. With care, he had named my mum.

When I left the service I went to Max. Though we hadn't met in fifty-five years, he knew who I was. We were both in tears, unable to find words. And there seemed so many words that were important to share. He hugged me warmly, offered me a history that Beryl had written of her life, then said, "This includes parts of your life. Perhaps you would like one for your brothers and sister?"

Outside the service, Max's wife, Wendy, asked what I thought of the service. The structure of the service I had found really helpful; the sermon I found distant, formulaic, and inappropriately evangelistic. "It is not what touches or nourishes people at a time like this."

Wendy agreed. Max's son Tim thought that the minister, being Beryl's minister, had the right to say it his way, and Wendy said that, "if he was Beryl's minister he could/should have shared more warmly about her."

I went to lunch with "my family." My dad had no brothers or sisters and his parents died so early. After my mum died we seemed to lose contact with the cousins in her part of the family. When I talked with Max, it was as though there were things that he had wanted to say to me ever since Elsie had died. "When Poppa Deadman (the father of Beryl and Elsie) died I was five," he said, "but I wasn't told that he had died, nor that my parents had gone to the funeral. I was dumped with someone. And when Elsie died I was not told that she had died." It was as though, with his mum's death, Max had the freedom to say things that he had wanted to say all these years. He invited Heather and me to come and stay with him in Tarrawingee on our trip south in June. In the conversation I mentioned that my younger brother, David, had been working to recall this period of his life and had been asking for help. Max said if it would help he would be willing to fly over to Perth (on the other side of the country,) to talk with him.

When I met Keith, I was trying to connect with him and with the death of his mother. "The last time I met your mum," I said, "she told me that you collected Australian art. Tell me about your art collection." It was probably an inappropriate question for the time and place, but how do you connect with a cousin you have not known in fifty-five years? The answer was warm and indicated that we had an interest in common.

I talked only briefly to Barbara (my aunt) saying something about it being hard when a sibling dies. I was much closer to Elsie," she said. "Beryl was thirteen and a half years older than me. There was a double bed and a single bed in our room at home. Beryl had the single bed and Elsie and I had the double bed. Beryl left home earlier. Wally and Elsie (my mum and dad) were my friends. I had saved about sixpence, and Wally took me into the city to buy Christmas presents. He spent about a pound buying presents for me to give to people." That's the spirit of my dad that I knew. It is the spirit that I know in my brother David, too.

When I drove home I was overwhelmed with deep tears. Probably it was dangerous to keep driving. In the book that Beryl had written were stories about Elsie. There were photographs of Elsie as a small child that I had never seen. I reflected on the connections, and the tears shuddered out of the deep parts of me. I had the sense that I had spent my life trying to create spaces in events like this, spaces where people could belong, and now somebody had done this for me. For fifty-five years I have longed for this sense of belonging in a family, and in this funeral something was set free for me and others.

ENSOULING

It was my sixtieth birthday on the weekend. More than seventy people came to our home for lunch. I love a party and I love providing thoughtfully prepared food for others. Smoked salmon and marinated chicken legs on one table, salt-crusted, garlic-infused roast beef and American ribs with chili on another. My family had had the piano tuned and brought in a pianist for the afternoon. They had wanted to surprise me. I wouldn't have guessed that they would do something like that in a hundred guesses. So when one of my sons asked "What's the music on the stereo Dad?" I said "Oh, that's a CD of Sydney jazz." "Is it? Go and have a look." I went and there was an unfamiliar man playing our piano.

Good food, lots of wine, piano sounds vibrating in the air around us, interesting people, and rich conversation. I wished I could be in all the conversations, but it is the nature of the thing when you host a party that you share a sentence here, half an idea there, a warm touch somewhere else . . . I enjoyed it all. When it was all done my body ached with tiredness. I lay on the bed my body wanting to sleep, my mind excited by the activity.

My wife and children had worked together to acknowledge my life: some ribbing, some fun, some critique, some acknowledgement—all in all a wonderfully alive expression of gratitude and love. What they said and how they said it was important to me beyond their naming. It was an "ensouling"—a nourishing of my soul. I have used the word to talk about what happens at a funeral when people talk of the life of the one who has died in a way that gives meaning to the life. I was influenced a few years ago when reading James B. Ashbrook's book *Minding the Soul*[1] to think that talking about someone's life in a meaningful way is to talk about that person's soul.

Over these last eighteen months I've felt as if my soul was being ripped apart by the theological college council's inability to acknowledge in any meaningful way my contribution to the seminary. And that makes me think of the Vietnam veterans returning to Australia and the United States in the 1970s and the silence that greeted them. Having responded to the call to serve their countries, they returned to little public recognition or acknowledgement. And subsequently many of them became ill, addicted, and directionless. Their souls were broken.

Enabling people to enter and leave communities in healthy, affirmed, and honest ways is very important. I have sought in ministry to say clearly "thank you" and "goodbye" when people leave a community. In the same way I have attempted to create space for people to join a community, to have access to the written and unwritten rules of the community, and to have their gifts acknowledged and used. Doing that contributes to the healthy ongoing function of individuals and community.[2] The party my family had organized was affirming me in a way that they knew to be really important. The people who came to share the day were joining in that affirmation.

So there I was, having cooked a dinner for seventy friends, including some from my new congregation, for I wanted to acknowledge their

1. Ashbrook, *Minding the Soul*.
2. See also Friedman, *Generation to Generation*.

hospitality in welcoming me as their minister, and to have them learn something about me and my family. I really enjoy sharing food with people, and the way that we divide domestic roles in our marriage, I do the cooking and Heather does the garden.

After we had eaten, my family called everyone together and then each in turn spoke with humor, joy, and appreciation about my life. My adult children had decided to talk about Doug the Artist, Doug the Turncoat and Name Dropper (I have changed my football team allegiance more than once, which is unforgivable in Australia), Doug the Cook, and Doug the Minister. They had had a longer list that they had fortunately edited—Doug the Tight-arse (even adult children can be irreverent with their father!), Doug the Academic, Competitive Doug Who Hates to Lose or Be Wrong, Doug the Camper, Doug the TV addict/TV Nazi, Doug the Friend, Doug the Father, and so on. They named their speech: "In the name of the father, the chef, and the sporting coach."

Heather talked about living with me, and the emergence over time of my gifts. There is an affirming pleasure for me in remembering the things she said, though I have to overcome the awkwardness of making them public. Looking back at her notes helped me recall. What Heather said contributed to the ensouling of me by talking about my life in a meaningful way. The people who gathered to listen by the very act of listening with interest also participated in the ensouling. Heather talked about things that she admired in me. She had a list: "emotional honesty, being a loving pastoral carer, a healer, a teacher, an artist at the cutting edge, and always making a community where everyone is valued and enabled to discover the religious in their own life's journey." She talked about how there was "no piety or bullshit, and an efficient use of time to fit in the game on TV, read a good book, and to enjoy good food, wine, coffee, and conversation." Then, Heather talked about what she saw as my most important traits: a passionate commitment to family life, parenting, and marriage. All things, if I am honest, that I needed and was glad to hear.

What stories others tell about you when you are present and listening always contributes to an understanding of your identity, and is often both different, and complementary, to the stories you tell your self.

As I look back on my journey of these last difficult years, this party was a high point. The ways my family named my life and achievements both professionally and as family person, the way my friends gathered and shared, the way we celebrated together seemed a really important event in moving on from the pain of being made redundant to discovering new purpose, new direction, and new ministry.

STATION 12, JESUS DIES

Memory finds its way to the surface of my life in so many unexpected ways.

It had been a really full-on week. I had contacted all the artists creating works for the Stations of the Cross project. The project is generating so much excitement, first among the artists who have been challenged by the questions put to them, and then by others around who see the possibilities of this project.

I had been able to contact all but one of the artists for the Stations project and, I thought that I might have to paint a work for his allocated station, Station 12, Jesus dies. (I really did not want to do this, because the project had to be about the work of others and not about me.) Nevertheless when I could not make contact with the artist I began to think about what I would do if I were to paint Station 12, Jesus dies. As I thought about it, I recalled standing over my dad's open coffin ten years earlier, and drawing his body. I decided that would make an interesting Station of the Cross. I eventually made contact with the artist; he just doesn't ever look at e-mail. He has his work well under way. I did not have to do anything, but I decided to make my station anyway. I found the drawing I had made in 1997 and made a painting from it. A couple of things surprised me: first, how quickly I found a method of working on the canvas that drew on the thousands of ink and wash figure drawings I have made in my sketch book, and second, how powerful was the image that emerged. Usually if I have tried to paint a face I can't find a satisfactory likeness. I always paint over what I create. This time both the likeness and the power amazed me. But the style is different from other paintings, but perhaps reflects my drawing both in sketchbook and from life.

The image is about my mortality. As my dad died, so I will die. There was no breath left in him. There will be no breath left in me. I am mortal. I have a limited time to live. One day my eyes will close and I will see no more. My breath will cease. My senses will no longer function. My body will be without life; it will turn to dust. I wonder how that awareness shapes my life and choices in the present?

8

Remembering

MEMORY

Not everything about ministry and priestly presence begins in the parish. Some begins in the family. My mother was cleaning out her home, aware that sometime in the future she might have to downsize. What should she keep? What should she throw away? What will the children want? What to do with the thousands of photographs my dad took, mostly of flowers? Who of the family will want, take, and look after these photographs?

The bigger and more threatening concern for my mum seems to be: "None of you children have indicated an interest in having your dad's photographs. Didn't you love him? What will happen to them? Should I just take them all out and burn them?" The underlying question of whether we loved Dad carries a good bit of uncertainty and pain. Then came a sequence of questions: "Why don't you want your father's photographs? Don't you value what he did with his life? Don't you want to value these artifacts?" and then, the questions turn back to reflecting on her own life and worth: "Who am I in this family? Who will value the photographs of my family of origin, of my childhood? How will I be remembered?"

That is the key question. How will we be remembered? Photographs become the memory of the family. We no longer have to trust our memory; we take photographs instead. When I gather with my adult children around the family table for a meal, someone will reach out to the nearby bookshelf and find a volume of family photographs. They will begin to flick through and remember. The photographs will stimulate stories. The partners of my children (and their children) are incorporated into the family by learning the stories, knowing the memory.

I have long been aware that in the latter part of their lives people need to revisit the photographs, the stories, and the memory of their lived experience in order to integrate their experience of living. When the stories are integrated or held together it is possible to live the next stage of life that in many cases is their dying.

When there were a few select photographs that documented family it was easy to keep them. However, my dad became a keen photographer. He photographed sunsets, almost daily when he lived overlooking the Indian Ocean where the sun set over the water lighting the sky with fabulous color. And he photographed indigenous wild flowers of Western Australia. He never discarded the lesser quality images. All were saved. The photographs might have been poetic metaphors interpreting his existence; the setting sun as he lived into his later years and the flowers that reflected the light, the color, the joy, and the hope that he always seemed able to find in life. He had a half dozen of his better images made into placemats that he marketed to raise funds for a hospice. I think all our extended family eats their meals using these placemats and the images are there to be seen and recognized. We all have memories of the man who took the photographs.

With the emergence of digital photography and phone cameras people are recording their lives in fractions of seconds. Click, click, click, click, click, click, click, and just a moment, could we please take another? Click. "Pass it across the table and let me have a look." The difficulty is in letting go the images, letting go the memory. Or, perhaps more to the point, what is it important that we remember?

In the previous story I told of how I had painted an image of my dad lying in his coffin. I sent a copy to my mother. Her first response by e-mail was "I don't need images of your dad to remember him. I remember the times we shared and the things that he said"; and she wrote about some of those things in detail. A few days later when I rang she thanked me for sending the image of the painting. I had forgotten that she had chosen not to see Wally's body after he had died, that she had said, "the body is just like a suitcase that carries the 'life' around. When the person dies the suitcase is discarded. It is not him." Now she told me, "I did not need to see it (the body). But your painting has been helpful because it has helped me to remember lots of things and so I have spent the last week remembering."

There remains this difficult question: how will my mother know the value of her life to us as her family if she thinks we do not have an interest in holding onto and valuing and keeping her memory?

In a related way, when I go to worship on Sunday, we, the gathered people (along with the gathered people all around the world,) read certain passages from the scripture. It is a form of communal memory. We remember who, and whose, we are when we read these stories. When we have listened to the stories we have someone, usually someone particularly equipped for the task, help us reflect on how the memory of the Christian tradition can shape our daily living. Our remembering is not restricted to words but comes also in ritual, symbol, music, and song, and it is natural that we should want to keep the memory alive.

Like my mother, I worry when I think that my children's generation has little or no interest in holding on to and valuing the memory of the faith community to which I belong. I am scared for a community that has been seduced by the ubiquitous camera into believing that they have no need for memory.

My role as priestly person, spiritual leader, and minister is to value (as sacred) the memory of individual and community. The family story remembered through the photographs shapes my identity too.

MY BROTHER'S REQUEST FOR HELP WITH HIS REMEMBERING

My younger brother David was going through a tough time. He asked me for some help. "I have no memories before I was about eight or nine. Can you help me remember? David's request to help him remember things about his early life meant that I kept reflecting, remembering, and writing. My second mother was also asking, "What can you remember of your birth mother?" Usually I responded "Quite a lot." For my brother, I began to write it down. While on the surface the writing of the memory was for my brother, clearly it was also for me. By remembering and telling the stories I am saying something really important that in the saying or telling shapes my priestly and pastoral identity. The stories need to be remembered and retold, for they shape identity.

After the funeral of my aunt, when my memory seemed to be enlivened about these things, I wrote to my brother telling him of the memories I had worked to hold on to over the years.

They are my memories, I said. They will at most be signposts to how I remember things that happened more than fifty-two years ago. They aren't right or wrong, just how I remember them. In sharing them with you, I hope they trigger your memories that may initially be like shadows drifting across the stage. And you'll possibly say, "I don't remember any of that. That's not how it was for me." And then (hopefully) one shadow suddenly gets some substance, some form, and it is yours (and no one else's).

There is no logical sequence to the things that I have written. They come as they came to mind. One memory seemed to bring another and another.

I drew and mailed to him a plan of the house we lived in as small boys. And I suggested he ask our older brother how he remembered the house. Down the back was a woodshed with a climbable persimmon tree on the house side, and a garage where the drive opened on to the side street.

Then I listed out a few pages of things that I remembered. Images of early childhood, places we traveled, things we did, the person and presence of our mum. And I sent them to him. It was good for me to write the things down and he told me that he found the list helpful.

I wrote to him: I have these memories in no particular order:

Being in the kitchen watching mum bathe you, and then in time, Joy, and my memories are particularly of her bathing Joy when she was a newborn in a metal tub, probably placed on the cream (?) kitchen table . . . the smells of soap and baby powder are strong for me . . . getting the water and the nappies ready, getting her dressed. It seemed a good sharing time.

And in the kitchen being with her while she prepared food. While we ate, Grahame would become a bit hungrier and be allowed to have a dripping sandwich. The dripping as I remember was kept in the fridge.

Elsie read us bedtime stories. I always liked the ones with nicely drawn pictures and I think that she bought us little Golden Books. There was always something to read. We had the books in our room.

I think that you had the bed closest to the back of the house, but maybe Grahame had that for some of the time too. I remember a few times getting into trouble from Mum for grabbing the bedroom curtains over the window between the beds and jumping onto the beds . . . trying unsuccessfully to swing like we had seen people do on ropes over the river.

I keep typing Elsie, but for this I want to say "Mum." We had two mothers. Elsie was our birth mother and Elizabeth our nurturing mother.

Mum would tuck us into bed and say two prayers with us: "Gentle Jesus meek and mild, look upon a little child, pity my simplicity, suffer me to come to thee. And God bless mummy and daddy, God bless my brothers and Joy, God bless my aunties and uncles and cousins and God bless my friends and God bless me." And perhaps the Lord's Prayer. Elizabeth, as a mother, taught us the Apostles' Creed, and the Hail Mary.

I remember Mum dressing us; getting us ready for particular outings; getting us ready for church. I remember being fascinated by the dust dancing in a sunbeam shining through the back window as we got ready.

I remember walking to church. The small fires burning the autumn leaves, and stopping off at a shop on the way home where you could get a homemade milk ice block for two-pence.

I remember Mum planting and growing pansies and poppies in the garden out the back door and near the swing.

And I remember Mum and Dad's energy for planting dahlias in the front garden and we all had to help . . . they had to be planted and later dug up and the bulbs kept in the wood shed until next year.

I remember Mum as a social person. We were allowed to stand in the doorway in our dressing gowns and watch as people came for a party.

I remember guests for Sunday tea shared around the table on the back verandah room.

I remember her contact with the neighbors. She knew the people next door and across the road in three directions and next door to them. The neighbors came into our home and she seemed welcome in theirs. I remember asking "Where is Mum?" and she was at the neighbors' and hadn't come home yet . . . probably, and here I am guessing, enjoying a cup of tea.

I remember picnics . . . at Howlong, at the Hume Weir, at the Waterworks, and in the Albury botanical gardens. On one of those picnics at Howlong, I think they had a portable radio and listened to Rosewell and Hoad playing the Davis Cup as nineteen-year-olds . . . so dramatic, so much tension in the commentary.

I remember Mum going to play tennis at the courts at the bottom of the Hill. She was serious about her tennis. I think Dad minded us while she played. But being with them at the courts (with their sand surface) she was more consistent hitting the ball to keep it in play. Dad was all big booming serve and not much else (in my memory).

I remember with you (I think) being taken to Albury Base Hospital to visit Mum before she died. I remember her frail body, trying so hard to reach out to us. You and I were under ten and one wasn't allowed to visit the hospital until one was ten years old. So we would probably not have seen mum in nine months and then, and I certainly was aware, so assume that someone had told me, that Mum was dying and this would be the last time we would see her. I talked with Grahame about this some years ago. I said how lucky he was that he could go and visit Mum in the hospital and he said, "No. You were the lucky ones. You were allowed to stay in the car and I had to go into the hospital and be with a woman who was my mother and who didn't recognize me."

I remember being welcome in their bedroom and playing games with both Mum and Dad in bed. I remember Mum sitting on her bed putting her stockings on. Think her side of the bed was furthest from the door.

This memory is a bit spookier: crawling on the floor under and behind the dressing table and there was a bag of something tied on the back of the dresser. We were told it was Mum's hair. I've always thought it odd that they collected her hair when it fell out having chemo, but now I think she probably, at some time, had her long hair cut and she kept the bits they cut off.

I remember Mum's crossness with me on a few occasions:

Dad and I were playing cricket along the back path with a leather cricket ball. He was trying to get me to play a straight bat. Well, I hit it straight and timed it well. It just didn't go along the ground but went through the window above the back door. Mum was pretty angry. We stopped the game.

I had been told never to run with sticks and not to run down hill and I ran down the hill with a stick, it caught between my legs, I went sprawling. It was near the bottom of the side street that I think was Sackville Street. Near the bottom on the right hand side going down was a big bullants nest. I lay there crying. I don't know how I got home but Mum had me in the laundry trough and she was delicately picking the ants from me. I recall she was displeased.

They were putting bitumen on the side street, and I was helping the men. I came home covered in tar. Mum had to go out and ask the men for some cloth and the spirits they used to get the tar off their bodies. Again I was stood in the trough, again she was displeased. The spirits stung, and I probably cried and she probably said, Serves you right. Listen and do as you are told.

I remember Mum rode in the front seat of the car with Dad . . . and Grahame always had the middle seat. This changed when Elizabeth became our mum; she sat next to Dad and Grahame now had the window seat.

I remember Mum encouraging me to paint. She (I assume) gave me a paint set and she set me up with brushes and water, told me how to use the paints, pointed me towards the landscape across the road, and said, paint. Other days she would encourage me to do coloring in. In the petrol stations you could get these C.O.R. coloring in things, and I would color them in. To this day I still wonder why the "neatest correct entry" would always win and that you didn't have much chance if you went over the lines. I liked going over the lines.

In the room that was the back verandah there was a table—probably the one from the kitchen. Mum would encourage us to play cubby houses putting blankets on the table to make walls and giving us kitchen pots and pans to have in our cubby house.

I remember visiting Beryl and Alan in Culcairn with Mum and Dad. I knew Beryl was Mum's sister and important. I knew these people as uncle and aunts, and Max and Kaye and Keith were our cousins. Our visits to them and their visits to us were special. I knew when Mum was with her family. There was a different sort of connection.

I remember a holiday at Bright on the Ovens River when we had adjoining units.

I remember trips to Sydney to visit her mum and dad's home. There, she was at home. There she belonged. There was a sense of excitement, joy, and ease in being in a place where she was so "known." I remember visiting Nanna (Wally's mum) in her home on one of those visits and as I remember it Mum did not come to Nanna's house.

I remember picnics at Carr's Park (in Blakehurst) in Sydney with her whole family: sister, brother, friends.

I remember her teaching us to ride her bike in the street outside our house . . . her lady's bike was a bit easier to ride. . . . And I remember the freedom she gave me to ride my bike to the baths and then, all over Albury and I still wasn't old enough to go to school.

I remember Mum taking me on the first day to Albury Infants School . . . and then trusting me to go on the bus.

I remember Sunday nights with Mum and Dad in the lounge room. After we were bathed and in our pajamas and dressing gowns, we would all go into the lounge-room, the fire going, jaffals for dinner cooked on the fire, slides or movies shown. There was a small green covered book in the lounge-room that had some paintings by aboriginal children as color images, and there were two black and white photographic prints of river gums hanging on the walls.

Then I begin to remember a Christmas morning shared as a family in that room around the Christmas tree. Mum and Dad were very generous to us kids at Christmas. I remember a cowboy tent, the indestructible carpet bowls.

I remember Mum pushing us on the swing out the back.

I remember crackers and bonfires on bonfire night, and I have a memory of her being angry with Dad for throwing crackers near us kids and scaring us.

I remember her joining us (not always) for a swim before breakfast at the Albury Pool.

After sleeping on it, a couple more memories:

Being at Albury Station early in the morning to say farewell to Grandma . . . a few visits come together as one memory. The crisp morning air (the train would leave at 8 a.m. I think), the people, all so busy, so focused. The stall where you could buy magazines and foods (and, when you and I traveled, the only time we were allowed to buy a comic). There would be noise: the hissing of steam, the clanking of carriages connecting up, the whistles of guards, and the bustling movement of the people. Mum and Dad would get on the train with us kids to settle Grandma in her seat. I would begin to get anxious that we'd be caught on the train after it had left. Dad would get off with us and Mum would stay with Grandma. The whistles would blow, the guard would be out with a flag, and Mum would still be on the train. I would get so worried about how far we'd have to drive to get her at the next station. Then, at the last moment she would get off. I would be enormously relieved. The train would slowly pull away, the continuous clanking of connections taking up the strain, clouds of steam, Grandma at the window waving, we running along the platform to wave goodbye.

After Mum died, one day Dad came to the school and picked us up and he took you and me to the Albury Cemetery to show us where they had buried Mum. We got there and there was a big mound of fresh earth, and a few flowers on top. I have the sense that some of the Deadman family was with us on this occasion. Certainly I remember there being a few extra people. I'm not sure whether Grahame went to Mum's funeral, but you and I didn't go. When, many years later, I asked Dad about why we didn't go to the funeral he was very clear, "Because I loved you and I thought it would be best for you not to go." It was a very intense experience for me. In 1968 (I think) I went to a conference at Tallangatta on the Hume Weir out from Albury. A friend was there with a car, and he drove me into Albury to find Mum's grave. Fourteen years had passed, and I could lead him straight to the cemetery and then in the general direction of where I thought the grave was in the cemetery, and there it was.

I also drew a plan of the house we lived in on the farm as I remembered it. To my brother I wrote: My memories are different of this home. I have, for example, little or no memory of being in the lounge-room and only faint memories of being in the dining room. The "rules" about where you could go in the home and what you could do there were quite different with Elizabeth as mother. In describing how they are different I do not mean in any way to be critical of Elizabeth as a mother. She learned her life differently from how Elsie learned her life. Mostly what we do when we create homes is copy the rules that existed in the houses in which we grew up because those rules, however logical or illogical, make us secure.

With Elizabeth, the lounge became a place for adults and special occasions, and that children were not allowed to enter; the dining room likewise. It is only in more recent years at Kings Park Avenue that I have felt free to enter Mother's lounge room without first asking. There were similar rules about entering the parents' bedroom and Joy's bedroom both on the farm and after that, so I have no idea of her room either.

These bits I put down to help you realize that the "rules" changed and it may be that you have little memory of those houses because you only went into a couple of rooms.

With Elizabeth as mother we were encouraged to be outside most of the time. We came inside to bathe, to eat, and to sleep. I recall sitting in the woodshed on the farm to read old newspapers because I wasn't allowed to read them inside.

9

Amen

BLESSING

THIS BOOK IS COMING to an end. There has been a journey through the stories that has reflected on identity, priestly presence, being a theological interpreter, memory, and identity. It is like leading worship. At the conclusion of worship there is a blessing of the people. To me, the blessing is a really important part of ministry, one that we sometimes undervalue.

My mother lives on the other side of the country. I call her every week and almost every week she finishes the conversation with the same words: God bless you, Doug." Sometimes I think I call her just to hear those words. They might on the surface sound clichéd or trite, but they are also a deep prayer, a special wish for God's goodness to rest upon me. A mother can say those words to her son. And I value them. I don't return them in kind. It would become trite or trivial. I accept the gift of her blessing but am not able easily to offer a blessing in return. For I am a son.

When my dad was dying, I flew to Perth and spent time with him in the palliative care ward. When I was leaving for what I thought would be the last time, I asked him if I could bless him. It was not easy to ask that question. Beside my dad's deathbed I was a son and not a minister or priest. I may have appeared calm on the surface, but internally I wrestled hard and long with the question: Am I a son or a priest? Is it appropriate for me to bless my dad? I remembered times my dad had ministered to me. At age eighteen when I was going out from the home to do examinations that would shape my life, and lead to my being able to follow my sense of call to ministry, my dad called the family together, said what an important day it was for me, and suggested that he pray for me. This was not the normal practice for our family, not the normal practice for my dad. We said grace at meals, but here he was reaching in to my space and my language and affirming who I was. It was a really important blessing of my life.

So many shared times remembered as I sat by his bed. Can I bless my dad? I wondered. Finally I found the courage to ask. I knew I had to return to my home in Sydney. "Dad, can I bless you?" I asked. "Yes, please," he said so clearly and warmly. So I reached out my hand and made the sign of the cross on his forehead, and through tears attempted to say the words of the Aaronic blessing: "The Lord bless you and keep you, the Lord make his face to shine upon you . . ." The words became jumbled; the tears fell on his bed. He looked up at me and said "Thank you." I walked away in the mysterious quiet of uncertainty.

I received a rather special gift in time. Dad outlived seventeen people in the palliative care ward, and was discharged to a nursing home. And, in the peculiarity that is life, I was invited to attend a national meeting of the church five hundred meters from the nursing home where he was now living. So I spent some of each morning being with him. Again I returned home. The parting was not so dramatic this time. He died twenty-four hours after the birth of his first great-grandchild.

I remember some special moments shared in ministry when people blessed me. Often it was in their journey towards death. Arnold died in his mid-fifties from cancer. He and his wife had been most caring of Heather and me in my first parish. I doubt that I would still be in ministry if they had not been there for me. They met with me weekly for half an hour to talk and pray at 6:30 every Friday morning. One morning as I was walking with them towards their car, Arnold turned to me and said, "The people of this parish do not know it, but you and Gray (the minister who had been in the parish before me) will both become national leaders in the Uniting Church." Somehow he offered a gift that affirmed my ministry at a time when I was making mistakes and struggling to live into my call and gift. He was right. We both became people who contributed to the national church.

Another day I was visiting with Pat. She was dying. It was the last visit I had with her. I prayed for her and for her family. When I finished my prayer she immediately prayed for me, asking God to bless my healing gifts. A wonderful blessing, and one always remembered because she died some hours later and there was a paradox between my presence with her in her dying and her acknowledgement of "my healing gifts."

There are other stories.

When I conduct a wedding I take time in the service to say to the congregation and to the couple that the one special thing that I do as a minister when I conduct your marriage (as contrasted to a civil celebrant) is that I bless you. So in the service when it comes to the moment of blessing I slow things down, I talk to the people: "What we do now is really special, we are going to bless, and I will mention the names of the couple who have just been married. I will use a really old blessing that comes from the Old Testament. They are simple words, repeated for probably twenty-five hundred years. Mystery, if you like; but in the saying of the words we together, are calling for, making a deep prayer, that the very best of God will rest upon this couple through their marriage.

I wonder how conscious people are of the importance of blessing in their lives. I wonder how often people are blessed.

As a pastor I visit the homes of the people in order to know them and to bless them. My prayer always includes a blessing of the home, of the people who live in it, of their children and grandchildren, and of all who might come into the home.

Blessing is, I think, "the work" of a priestly person or a spiritual leader. It comes from who you are more than what you do. It is paradoxically simple. Anyone can say the words "God bless you." The words carry something extra when they are brought by a spiritual leader, a priestly person, whose lived life reflects the discipline of the calling.

In the introduction to this book I mentioned the conversation with my colleague, Bill, who was invited to become a theological educator full time but he said no, because he would lose the opportunity to bless the people.

I understand this now in ways that I haven't before. When I lead worship the most important thing I do is to bless the people at the conclusion of the service. The final benediction. I stand and raise my hand make the sign of the cross and say, "The blessing of God the Creator, the son and the Spirit, be and remain with you always." And the people sing the refrain, "Amen, Amen, Amen."

We all need to be blessed, and one of the most significant things that I do as a spiritual leader or priestly person is to bring a blessing, to say in simple ways that what I wish for the people is that the fullness, the richness, the possibility of God might be with them in all of their living.

A MINISTRY-SHAPING PRAYER

I was out walking through the local creek valley, thinking about all that had happened. It is a deep gorge, carved by hundreds of years of intense storm run off. We had had heavy storms in the previous week and I was intrigued with just how much water had been running through the valley. The bent over trees and the detritus that was caught was way above my normal walking path.

I was thinking about anything and everything. I thought of the cousins that I had stayed with on my previous week's holiday. These were conversations that had waited fifty-five years to happen. Suddenly it jumped into my mind that my parents had had me pray for these cousins when I was a small child.

I began to recall the prayer that I shared with my brother. My parents would sit on my or my brother's bedside at the end of the day and teach us to pray:

"God bless . . ."

Probably it was the result of getting towards the end of this book, and of the other things that I have written about the importance of being able to bless people that I began to realize that from early childhood my parents had helped me develop a practice that would be core to the ministry that I would live. Through that prayer they were helping me develop the practice of asking God to bless the people, individually and communally. It is what I do when I visit the people in homes and hospitals; it is what I do at the end of worship and gatherings; it is what I do in weddings and baptisms and funerals. It is what I do as a priestly person. It is priestly presence.

This practice of prayer has shaped my life and ministry.

I will always be grateful to those who helped me develop the practice of prayer and blessing that formed for the ministry I have been so privileged to live.

10

Where Am I Now?

On the day that I went to St. Ives to talk with the congregation about the possibility of becoming their minister, two friends rang me, one from interstate and the other from overseas. Both encouraged me in similar ways: "In each place that you have been in ministry before, you have done things that you could not have anticipated when you first went there. New things have happened."

Certainly that has been so in St. Ives. We have completed a second Stations of the Cross project. There was a great deal of interest and excitement around it. The people responded with a new excitement as they approached Easter and the exhibition. At the same time we are planning a new Advent program: Stations of Creation. We have shaped fifteen stations of creation and birth from the biblical stories and have invited fifteen composers each to create a new piece of music in response to the particular stations. The works will be performed in an Advent Concert. This program builds on the program of special concerts that have been run by the church for a number of years.

In another area of ministry, the congregation's long-term vision to do something to address the hidden pain of domestic violence in the community was funded. So we have appointed a senior's worker whose responsibility is to help in the prevention of elder abuse.

I recall that on the day I was told that my position in theological education had been made redundant, one of my sons said to me, "Dad, one of the things that will happen is that your identity will take a battering—because your identity is so much tied up with what you do." At the time I thanked him, and with parental arrogance, thought under my breath "I know that." But I didn't know that. I didn't know just how deeply the losing of my role as an academic, a thinker on behalf of the church, one who was involved in forming people for ministry, and the status shaped by those functions would effect my person. I didn't know how dark the darkness would be. Ever since being made redundant I had a strong need to reaffirm what I perceived as my identity, by telling stories about it. Over and over I found myself telling people stories that were affirming my identity. I needed to let people know who I was. In telling these stories I was becoming clearer about my own identity.

My identity had been turned upside down and inside out. I would drive to church to lead worship on Sunday morning almost shouting at my self: "I am the minister of this congregation, these people have been given to my care, I am to love the people given to my care. My responsibility is to lead the best worship I can lead, to preach with integrity. That is who I am, that is what I do." As I have written this book I have told and retold stories of my life, stories that shape my identity as priestly person, stories that reflect on the practice of ministry. The telling of these stories in this way has been really helpful in reintegrating who I am. The storytelling has put back together what has been pulled apart. The reclaiming of identity has been reclaiming who I am as husband, father, friend, artist, writer, thinker, pastoral theologian, and priestly person.

The Stations of the Cross project has had an interesting part in all of this. It has sharpened my awareness that life is journey. Also that I am mortal, finite, and one day will die. I am aware that I, like the people around me, stumble under the knowledge of that mortality, that at times life strips us bare, but also that there are people along the way to help. And somewhere there is the promise and hope of resurrection. Life is greater than me; not too long after I have died, what I have done and who I am will be quickly forgotten, but the gospel will continue to be proclaimed and the people will continue to gather to worship and serve God.

A gift of the Stations project is that I have gone to visit the artists in their studios, and I call that "work"! The first thing that happened to me was that I realized that my paintings weren't good enough. I didn't push hard enough to make good paintings. Perhaps that was similar to when I first entered theological education and had to learn to think harder and write with more discipline. What I learned about my painting was that I had to push harder, to find the simple mark that would say more things. That was also true in my preaching; could I consciously say less to express more? I think that I am. After more than a year of real uncertainty as an artist, I think I have begun to find a tighter, tougher, more refined way of creating images that reach further and deeper in the viewer. My artist friends are seeing that too.

I have come to realize more clearly that artists address their lived experience in answering the questions posed by the Stations of the Cross.

A couple of weeks ago I stood with Euan Macleod in his studio looking at his work for the Stations 2008. He had been allocated station 14, Jesus is laid in the grave.

Euan is always addressing "existential anxiety" when he paints. The question is always there: what does it mean to "be"? Who are we in our frail bodies and minds against the stability of land and sea?

The images he so frequently paints are shaped by his dad's having had Alzheimer's for ten years before he died at an early age. Somehow resolving what it meant for him that his dad was ill and died has shaped and continues to shape Euan's painting. In his paintings he often paints a large shadowy male figure and a boat, both against the landscapes of New Zealand, the place of his birth, and of central Australia.

The boat that he uses is ambiguous. His dad had built a boat in their lounge room and when he died after ten years of suffering with Alzheimer's, his mother put the open coffin in the lounge room. The boat and the coffin had become the same thing. And so in Euan's paintings the symbol of the boat is a kind of counterpoint to "being" when it appears.

In the paintings that he has done for the Stations project, he has two paintings for station number 14:

One painting has a shadowy figure standing over a draped corpse. There are curtains partly covering the window and then they open to expose a feminine landscape, which is the view from his mother's window. The land could be read as large breasts. It is, he said, the landscape of his mother. The second painting—he wants the two hung together—is of a much clearer figure hunched, bent at the shoulders, pushing the boat, which is filled with a naked man/corpse lying as in a coffin, his genitals visible, exposed. The boat is being pushed out onto the waters. Across the bay is a landscape that Euan grew up with and which he has painted many times—his dad's landscape. There are so many questions in these paintings—all about this "existential anxiety."

Paul Tillich[1] wrote *The Courage to Be* as a response to the questions raised for him by existential anxiety. Rollo May[2] wrote *The Courage to Create* in response to Tillich's *The Courage to Be*." Euan McLeod looks, experiences, wonders, and paints in ways that similarly address the deep questions shaped by the anxiety of being. The answers don't come easily.

1. Paul Tillich, *The Courage to Be*.
2. Rollo May, *The Courage to Create*.

They are beyond words: that is why he paints. Perhaps all that he does in his paintings is to hold up the important questions. The questions come through in the way he depicts the figure; the tension for the figure is always portrayed against the stability and permanence of the land and sea.

It is this engagement of integrity with the deep questions of being that reinforces something of the importance for me of being present to all the people in the vulnerable, fractured, and uncertain times of their living. That is what I am called to be and do.

I am happy in what I do. It is a privilege to be invited into people's homes and the intimate moments of their lives. When I was in theological education one of the things I found hardest was that I rarely went into the homes of other people.

I enjoy immensely preaching to a receptive and appreciative community. The worship I lead is shaped by my visiting and "knowing" of the people. I think the people know that too, and they trust me and what I bring. The discipline of praying a passage of scripture each week in such a way that I allow it to be inside me and I inside it, in order that I can speak it in a relevant and meaningful way nourishes my (faith) life.

Of course I am still hurt and confused when I think of the events that surrounded how my position was made redundant. I still have great difficulty being in the presence of people who I think acted without integrity. I do not wish to be like that. I want to move on. I wrote earlier of the day there was an important change inside me, and I threw out sixteen years of teaching notes. I was saying to myself, this is not how I want to be known. It reminded me of the day I threw out the sporting trophies that had I won in my youth. That is no longer how I see myself. Those actions made a difference.

Another thing that made a difference was the sermon that I preached (really to myself and that the congregation overheard) on the line in the Lord's Prayer "as we forgive those who sin against us." It led to our shaping a new liturgical response to the prayer of confession. We conclude the prayer with these words:

> *God give us the grace to forgive those who have hurt us.*
>
> *Enable us to provide a space for those whom we have offended to forgive us.*
>
> *May we be a forgiven and forgiving people.*
>
> *By the grace of God. Amen.*

Where Am I Now? 163

This wasn't just for me. I knew that others in the congregation carried deep hurts from the ways in which they had been treated in the past and I wanted the liturgy to help them live abundantly too.

I also enjoy immensely the times when people come forward to the front of the church to receive the elements of bread and wine at communion. This is not the only way we receive the elements, but when we do I stand in the center of the front of the church and give the people the bread. I call each person by name and place the broken bread in his or her hands. And in the pronouncing of the name there is unspoken an acknowledgement of all that I know about this person. It is a priestly action of blessing.

Being able to bless the people is a privilege of pastoral ministry. At the conclusion of worship, from behind the table around which we have gathered, with my arms open and outstretched, I say words of mission. Then I make the sign of the cross with my right hand, and say, "The blessing of God, Creator, Son, and Spirit, be with you now and forever." It is the same every time. I want there to be a sameness in this blessing so that the people know it deeply in their hearts. And in response they sing, "Amen, Amen, Amen."—let it be so.

Appendix

HERE ARE A NUMBER of questions that you might take slowly, one at a time, to reflect on in order to shape your life and ministry.

- What do these call stories evoke in you?
- What are the call stories that shape who you are?
- What does your life call out in you?
- How have you "heard a voice" in your life? Where and when and what did it call you to? If you haven't "heard a voice," what has shaped the direction of the call on your life?
- How have others affirmed your gifts and directed you towards specific tasks in your life?
- What are the times when "life" has conspired against what you feel your life calls out in you? Go slowly and describe the time and what happened within you.
- How have you coped with/moved beyond that difficult time?
- How would you name your life goals? What values shape your life goals?
- How have those goals changed at different key points in your life?
- How do you discern the way to go forward at key crossroads in your life?
- How do you understand the role and function of a "priestly person/spiritual leader?"
- What times, places, practices do you use to develop your capacity to "be?"
- What do you do when there is nothing that you can do (other than be present to the moment)?
- What is your prayer discipline? How might you develop it further?
- How do you meet your needs for intimacy?
- What do you do for the nourishment of your body? Your soul?

Your intimate relationships?
- What disciplines do you have for attending to the lived experience of the "other?"
- What experiences have reshaped your understanding of your identity? What stories would you tell of these times? How has that shaped and reshaped your understanding of who you are and what you do?
- In what ways do you structure "thinking time" into your working week?
- If you lead worship, preach sermons, or teach, how do you prepare for these tasks? Go slowly and list the various parts in the process. What new things could you do that might enhance the process?
- What creative texts do you listen to (music, theater, movies, books, art in museums, etc.)?
- What are your places for, and practices of, play?
- How do you reflect theologically on the things happening around you?
- How do you discern the voice of God in the lived experience of the people around you?
- Where do you see hope breaking free in the world?
- What is your hope?
- What are your disciplined "practices of faith"?
- What are the times in your life when you have experienced the blessing of another person? What form did that blessing take? How has the blessing shaped who you are?
- What are the times when you have blessed another? What do you think happens in the moment of blessing? How important is it for you?
- How do you discern the presence and voice of God in the lived experience of the people around you?
- How do you understand "soul"?
- Can you recount times and experiences of "ensouling"?

- Who are the people who have prayed for your life? What do you think was the form of their prayer?
- What are the times of retreat that you share? With whom do you share retreat? How intentional are those times?
- What are the times of greatest uncertainty for you? How do you survive in those times?
- How do you deal with your experiences of loneliness?
- How do you set boundaries in your living? Are those boundaries appropriate?
- Have there been times for you when you had to choose between life and death? How did you choose life?
- In what moments of your life have you found light emerging from the darkness?

Bibliography

Ashbrook, James B. *Minding the Soul*. Minneapolis: Fortress, 1996.
Bilman, Kadi, and Dan Migliore, *Rachel's Cry*. Cleveland: United Church Press, 1990.
Brueggemann, Walter. *The Message of the Psalms*. Minneapolis: Augsburg, 1984.
Collis, Jack. *One Life to Live*. Essendon: Pennon, 2004.
Dykstra, Craig. "Pastoral and Ecclesial Imagination." In *For Life Abundant: Practical Theology, Theological Education, and Christian Ministry*, edited by Dorothy C. Bass and Craig Dykstra, 41. Grand Rapids: Eerdmans, 2008.
Emerson, J. G. *The Dynamics of Forgiveness*. London: George Allen and Unwin, 1965.
Friedman, Edwin H. *Generation to Generation*. New York: Guildford Press, 1985.
Ghiselin, Brewster. *The Creative Process: A Symposium*. Berkeley and Los Angeles: University of California Press, 1952.
Holliday, J. E., ed. *The RAAF POWs of Lamsdorf*. Darlinghurst: Alpha Biomedical Communications, 1992.
Lischer, Richard. *Open Secrets: A Spiritual Journey through a Country Church*. New York: Doubleday, 2001.
May, Melanie A. *A Body Knows*. New York: Continuum, 1995.
May, Rollo. *The Courage to Create*. New York: Norton, 1975/94.
Neumark, Heidi B. *Breathing Space: A Spiritiual Journey in the South Bronx*. Boston: Beacon Press, 2003.
Purnell, Douglas. *Conversation as Ministry: Stories and Strategies for Confident Caregiving*. Cleveland: Pilgrim, 2003.
Roskill, Mark, ed., *The Letters of Vincent Van Gogh*. New York: Atheneum, 1985.
Sung Park, Andrew. *The Wounded Heart of God*. Nashville: Abingdon, 1993.
Tillich, Paul. *The Courage to Be*. New Haven: Yale University Press, 1952/80.

www.ingramcontent.com/pod-product-compliance
Lightning Source LLC
Chambersburg PA
CBHW071231170426
43191CB00032B/1312